THE BIG BOOK OF IQ TESTS

HOW SMART ARE YOU?

THE BIG BOOK OF IQ TESTS

NORMAN SULLIVAN

PHILIP J. CARTER

**BLACK DOG
& LEVENTHAL
PUBLISHERS**
NEW YORK

This 1998 edition is published by arrangement with
Sterling Publishing Company, Inc. by

Black Dog & Leventhal Publishers, Inc.
151 West 19th Street
New York, NY 10011

Distributed by

Workman Publishing Company
708 Broadway
New York, NY 10003

Manufactured in China

ISBN: 1-57912-022-9
h g f e

CONTENTS

Variety is the spice of life, and our aim in putting together this compilation has been to include as wide a variety of puzzles, representing a wide range of difficulty, as possible. You may find some of the questions easy to answer, while others will tax you beyond your limits—that's okay! The challenge is part of the fun, and you'll certainly find that as you progress through the book, you'll sharpen your ability to solve problems and exercise your brain in new and exciting ways. Think of your mind as a muscle, and of these tests as your "exercise regimen." The more you work out, the stronger you get. And the stronger you are, the more fun your workout becomes.

Here's a little background on some of the puzzle types included in this book.

PUZZLES OF THE MIND

These puzzles consist entirely of diagrammatic representation. To solve them, you have to apply your mind to each set of diagrams, comprehend the experience before you, and decide what logical patterns and/or sequences are occurring. The puzzles do not involve numeracy or literacy, but are purely exercises of the mind, designed to test raw intelligence, free from the influence of prior knowledge.

GAMBLING AND PROBABILITY

The urge to defeat the laws of probability is inherent in most people, although it was not until the 17th century, when Blaise Pascal, a French mathematician formulated the first rules relating to probability, that people were really aware that they existed.

It was in 1654 that the Chevalier de Méré asked Pascal why he lost when he bet even money that a pair of sixes would show once in 24 rolls of the dice. Pascal demonstrated that 24 rolls would be against the gambler, but 25 rolls could be slightly in his favor.

In America during the gold-rush era, a very ingenious gambling game garnered a lot of money for its perpetrators. Three cards were placed in a hat: one card was gold on both sides, one card was silver on both sides, and one card was gold on one side and silver on the other side. The gambler would take one card and place it on the table showing gold on the back of the card. Then he would bet the onlookers even money that gold would be on the reverse side, his reasoning being that the card could not be the silver/silver card, therefore there were only two possibilities: gold/silver or gold/gold. A fair and even bet—or is it?

The catch is that the game involves *sides,* not cards. We start with six sides, three gold and three silver. We eliminate the silver/silver card and we can see one gold side. That leaves two gold and one silver unseen. Odds are therefore 2-1 that the reverse side is gold. The basic rule is really quite simple. Calculate the chances that an event will happen and then calculate the chances that it will not happen. Example: What are the odds against drawing a named card out of a pack of 52?

The probability of drawing the right card is $1/52$. The probability of not drawing the right card is $51/52$. The odds in favor of drawing the right card is the ratio of the first probability to the second, that is, $1/52$ to $51/52$, or 1 to 51.

CROSSWORDS

On Sunday, December 21, 1913, the first crossword puzzle appeared in the *New York World*. It was devised by Liverpool-born Arthur Wynne, who called it a Word Cross Puzzle. Now, of course, crosswords are a favorite of puzzlers worldwide.

CRYPTOGRAMS

A cryptogram is a puzzle in which one letter is substituted for another. How does one go about decoding a cryptogram? The easiest to deal with are those that contain a four-letter word beginning and ending with the same letter, e.g., FGHF. This is almost certainly the word THAT, which should enable you to discover the word THE, and now you're well on your way to solving the cryptogram.

Knowledge is continually being updated in the fields of letter frequency, word frequency, most common word endings, and the like. For example, the order in which letters appear most frequently in English today is ETAOINSRHLDCUMFPGWYBVKXJQZ.

The majority of cryptograms are simple types, where each letter of the alphabet is substituted for another, and there is only one message to be decoded. But what if the sender of the message wishes to convey a further message within the same cryptogram? This is done by the addition of keywords, which may be hidden in either the plain or the keyed text. As all the cryptograms in this book have keywords or keyed phrases, we can show how these are uncovered by means of the following comment from Oliver Hardy, which he made to explain why he thought people found the Laurel-and-Hardy partnership so funny.

G LZOKK GI BRK SOPRZKO BO BOHO KM PMFX-WOIOWD ZQWGVO GQ OAOHD BRD. SZI, WGVO SRPMQ RQN OLLK, BO KOOFON IM SO RSMZI XOHTOPI IMLOIJOH—SZI QMI KM LMMN RXRHI.

This is a simple substitution cryptogram, where one letter of the alphabet has been substituted for another, and is therefore deciphered in the usual way.

I GUESS IT WAS BECAUSE WE WERE SO COMPLETELY UNLIKE IN EVERY WAY. BUT, LIKE BACON AND EGGS, WE SEEMED TO BE ABOUT PERFECT TOGETHER—BUT NOT SO GOOD APART.

To find the keyed quotation place the code text in juxtaposition to the plain text, thus:

(Plain Text)

A B C D E F G H I J K L M N O P Q R S T U V W X Y Z
R S P N O T L J G V W F Q M X H K I Z A B   D

(Code Text)

As nothing appears yet which might look like a message, arrange the code text alphabetically in juxtaposition to the plain text:

(Code Text)

A B C D E F G H I J K L M N O P Q R S T U V W X Y Z
V W Y M I R T H S G O D E C N A B F   K L P U

(Plain text)

Usually the keyword or, in this case, the keyed quotation, contains the only letters which do not appear in alphabetical order. By inspecting the plain text, you may easily pick out where the alphabet appears in orderly succession and thus isolate the keyword letters. Above we see A to Y in order, thus suggesting the keyed quotation is contained in the letters MIRTHS-GODECN. Because letters cannot be repeated in simple cryptograms, the fun begins if the keyed quotation repeats letters. It is therefore necessary to use your imagination to make sense of the message. In this case the answer is MIRTH IS GOD'S MEDICINE.

The addition of keywords has several purposes, in addition to the practical one of sending an additional message that may escape the attention of an interceptor. It gives the compiler an opportunity to comment on the coded material, which is usually a quotation, and to display his own wit as he adds an extra dimension to the puzzle.

ANAGRAMS

Anagrams were invented by the Greek poet Lycophon in 280 A.D. Originally, an anagram was simply a word which, when reversed, formed another word. For example, ROOM/MOOR or TIDE/EDIT. The word "anagram" is derived from the Greek: "Ana" means backwards and "Gramma" a letter.

The best anagrams are those in which the rearranged letters bear some relationship to the original word or name; for example, the letters of the word "SOFT-HEARTEDNESS" can be rearranged to form the phrase "OFTEN SHEDS TEARS."

Now you're ready to begin. Suggested time limits are included at the beginning of each group of questions. You can use these to challenge yourself, or you can ignore the time constraints completely and work through the problems at your own rate. Scoring guidelines appear at the end of each section. The chart matching your composite score with an IQ equivalent score is a loose assignment of an "IQ score" and is not Mensa-approved. Again, these are only guidelines: you are the best judge of your own success. Have fun!

GROUP I

ELEMENTARY LEVEL

I MISSING SQUARE

Study the diagram and decide what logically should be the missing section from the choices given.

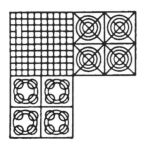

Choose from:

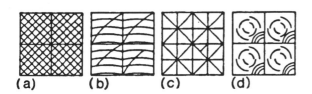

(a)   (b)   (c)   (d)

2 LOGIC

Find the next figure:

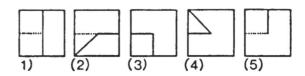

1)   (2)   (3)   (4)   (5)

Choose from:

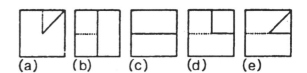

(a)   (b)   (c)   (d)   (e)

3 TYPIST

A typist types four envelopes and four letters. She places the letters in the envelopes at random. What are the chances that only three letters are in their correct envelopes?

4 LUCKY CARD

In a competition, each person receives a card with a number of rub-off pictures. One picture is marked "loser," and only two pictures are identical. If the two identical pictures appear before the picture marked "loser" does, then the competitor wins a prize.

There are 60 pictures on the card. What are the odds against winning?

5 WORD CROSS PUZZLE

This puzzle is based on the first crossword by Arthur Wynne.

ACROSS

2 Human being (3)
4 Give rise to (5)
6 Assembled (7)
8 Animal (4)
9 Vivacity (4)
11 Actor's part (4)
12 Falsehoods (4)
14 Greek letter (4)
15 Marsh plant (4)
16 Adorn (4)
18 Adjacent (4)
19 Page (4)
21 Imitates (4)
22 Parts of coat (7)
24 Parts of body (5)
25 Not high (3)

DOWN

1 Story (4)
2 Only (4)
3 Knob (4)
4 Expose (4)
5 Explain (4)
6 Spacious buildings (7)
7 Milk suppliers (7)
8 Inn (5)
10 Requires (5)
11 Color (3)
13 Look With Eyes (3)
17 Vegetable (4)
18 Spill Out (4)
20 Tumbled (4)
21 Profess (4)
23 Made of Ebony (4)

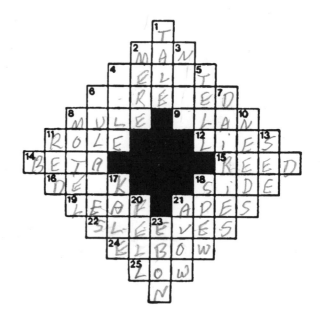

6 MAGIC SQUARES

Here are five connected 5 × 5 magic squares. Answers are all five-letter words, and each of the five grids reads the same both across and down.

CLUES

1 Faded
2 Sky blue
3 Money
4 Made mistakes
5 Actions
6 Swap
7 Made angry
8 Excuse
9 Sum owed
10 Shortens
11 Express
12 Teacher
13 Make amends
14 Medicine
15 Set upright
16 Shot at billiards
17 Pains
18 Makes purchases
19 Color
20 Composition
21 Vagabond
22 Runner
23 Sharp
24 Gives out
25 Force

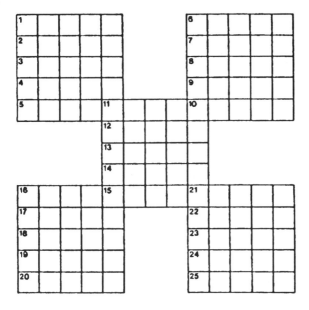

7 CRYPTOGRAM

Message keyed, 10-2-4-6

SNL NQGCF SHZC T MHTK GN JNY GSHG LSCF
JNY SHZC CDTETFHGCK GSC TEWNMMTODC,
LSHGCZCI ICEHTFM, SNLCZCI TEWINOHODC,
EYMG OC GSC GIYGS?
KNJDC

8 CRYPTOGRAM

Message keyed, 4-3-4

ME MR SQAHQ EA ZPQJ ELPE HO QOON
RAYMEFNO EA VMQN AFDROYGOR. BODLPBR ME
MR QAE RA HOYY SQAHQ ELPE HO QOON
RAYMEFNO EA VMQN AFD VOYYAHR OGOQ ELO
RPGMAD MR NORUDMTON PR DOPULMQW
ZPQSMQN ELDAFWL ELO HMYNODQQRR.
LPGOYAUS OYYMR

9 PHONE NUMBER

This was my old telephone number. What does it remind you of?

(314)159-2654

10 EXPLORER

Base to explorer at the South Pole:

"What's the temperature?"

"Minus 40 degrees" says the explorer.

"Is that Centigrade or Fahrenheit?" asks base.

"Put down Fahrenheit," says the explorer. "I don't expect it will matter."

Why does he say that?

11 LOGIC

What is the next logical number in this sequence?

3, 7, 10, 11, 12, ?

12 PRODUCT

Find the product of:

(x-a) (x-b) (x-c) ... (x-z)

13 BARTENDER

Two strangers enter a bar. The bartender asks them what they would like. The first man says, "I'll have a bottle of beer," and puts 50 cents down on the counter.

Bartender: "Miller at 50 cents, or Budweiser at 45 cents?"

First man: "Budweiser."

Second man: "I'll have a bottle of beer," and he puts 50 cents on the counter. Without asking him, the bartender gives him a Miller. How did he know what the man wanted?

14 WAITER!

A man calls to a waiter, "There's a fly in my tea".

"I will bring you a fresh cup of tea," says the waiter.

After a few moments the man calls out, "This is the same cup of tea!" How did he know?

15 ANAGRAM PHRASES

Each word or phrase in quotation marks is an anagram of another word. The solution bears some relationship to the original.

(a) "UP CLOSE" "TRIFLING" (7/8)
Answer: "_____" "_____"

(b) "EMIT GRUNT" through "MOUTH CASE" (9/9)
Answer: "_____" through "_____"

16 ANIMALGRAMS

The following are all anagrams of animals:

(a) CORONA
(b) PAROLED
(c) RETIRER
(d) LESIONS
(e) SOMEDAY
(f) ALPINES
(g) ORCHESTRA
(h) CALIFORNIA (two words)

17 THREESOMES

(a) These two four-figure numbers share a feature in common with only one other four-figure number. What is the feature and what is the other number?

3600, 5776

(b) These two four-figure numbers share a feature in common with only one other four-figure number. What is the feature and what is the other number?

2025, 9801

18 SENTENCES

Which one of these sentences is the odd one out?

(1) FRIENDSHIP LINGERS UNTIL THE END.
(2) LOVERS STROLL UNDER THE STARS.
(3) HEAVEN ALWAYS REPAYS PERFECTION.
(4) THE UPROAR BEGINS AGAIN.

19 CLASSIFICATION

An intelligence test in which you are shown a number of boxes and asked to choose the one which is different is called "Classification." Which one of the following boxes is the odd one out?

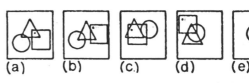

(a)　(b)　(c.)　(d)　(e)

20 WHAT! NO VOWELS

Work from the top left-hand square to the bottom right, moving from square to square horizontally, vertically or diagonally, to find five words. Every letter in the grid must be used once only.

start

C	Y	P	N	M
H	R	T	N	Y
Y	R	S	H	Y
M	T	T	Y	M
H	T	R	P	H

finish

21 CUCKOO IN THE NEST

Each of the sentences below contains, in the correct order, the letters of a word that is opposite to the meaning of the sentence, e.g. **CL**O**SE TO** BO**IL**ING = COOL .

Find the words:

(a) A HAVEN OF LOVELINESS
(b) NOT FOR SOME TIME OR MAYBE NEVER
(c) FROZEN, NOT OFF THE SHELF
(d) A GREAT EFFORT AND STILL FRESH ENOUGH TO DO IT OVER AGAIN
(e) PUT YOUR EFFORT IN SHIFTING IT TOWARDS US
(f) SEW IT VERY TIGHTLY TOGETHER
(g) A LOT OF COMPANY FOR ME
(h) HATED OR REVILED
(i) READ IN COMPLETE SILENCE TO YOURSELF
(j) INDELICATE, UGLY AND UNCULTURED
(k) TRUSTY, EVER SINCERE AND HONEST
(l) NEW AND INEXPERIENCED MEMBER OF OUR BODY AND PROFESSION
(m) RUN ALONG SPEEDILY IN THE RACE
(n) NOW STALE AND VERY WORN

22 SISTERS

Coincidence seems to run in our family. Although my sisters Pam and Fran each have five children, twins and triplets, Pam had her twins first, whereas Fran had triplets first.

I saw Pam the other day, and she remarked that the sum of the ages of her children was equal to the product of their ages. I pointed out that although interesting, this was not unique, as Fran could say exactly the same about her children.

How old are my sisters' children?

23 ZERO

Without changing the order of the digits, insert four plus signs, one division sign, and three minus signs between them to make the calculation correct.

9 8 7 6 5 4 3 2 1 = 0

24 FAMILY WAY

My two uncles and five cousins were all born on different days of the week. Uncle Alan was born on a Friday and his daughters, my cousins Judith and Mary, were born on a Monday and Saturday respectively. My other uncle, Paul, was born on a Sunday and his eldest son, my cousin Richard, was born on a Thursday. His other sons, Roy and Terry, were born on the two remaining days of the week; but which one was born on a Tuesday and which one was born on a Wednesday?

25 THE MEETING

The man from the country at the top of the Himalayas came by plane to meet the man from the Far East, who was wearing a chain around his neck. What was the weather when they met the man from the Middle East?

26 MISSING SQUARE

Find the missing square:

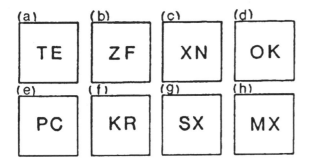

FR	NE	TO
TE	FE	SN
ET	OE	

Choose from:

(a) TE	(b) ZF	(c) XN	(d) OK
(e) PC	(f) KR	(g) SX	(h) MX

27 LAUGHING MATTER

All these words are connected with humor:

(a) _H_M_Y

(b) _L_P_T_C_

(c) _A_T_R

(d) _A_I_A_U_E

(e) _U_F_O_E_Y

(f) _U_L_S_U_

(g) _O_U_A_I_Y

(h) _P_O_

(i) _A_I_A_E

(j) _A_I_E

(k) _A_C_

(l) _A_T_O_

(m) _O_X

(n) _O_E_Y

NOW CHECK YOUR ANSWERS AND RECORD YOUR SCORE.

1 Pair words in the first column with words in the second column, finishing with nine pairs.

(1) TENNIS   (A) WORK
(2) SAFETY   (B) STORE
(3) HOUSE   (C) CLAD
(4) SHOP   (D) BENCH
(5) SEE   (E) MATCH
(6) BAND   (F) LOCK
(7) IRON   (G) SAW
(8) WORK   (H) AGE
(9) TOY   (I) HOLD

2 Which of these wrought-iron gates differs from the others?

3 What two terms complete this series?

A I D 4 H 8 M 13 – –

4 What names are these?

(A) O P S N B O
(B) K T K U
(C) D Q Q H
(D) V M G L E V H

5 Which is the odd one out?

(A) GRAND
(B) TEN-SPOT
(C) BUCK
(D) RAND
(E) C-NOTE

6 Which scroll is wrong?

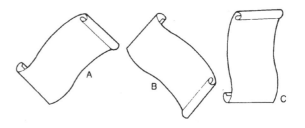
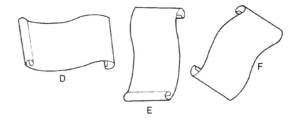

7 Assuming four of these dates are correct, which one is wrong?

(A) SATURDAY, JANUARY 7, 1764
(B) SATURDAY, JANUARY 21, 1764
(C) SATURDAY, FEBRUARY 11, 1764
(D) SATURDAY, MARCH 11, 1764
(E) SATURDAY, APRIL 14, 1764

8 Which is the odd one out?

(A) CONSTABLE
(B) ABATTOIR
(C) REBATE
(D) COMBATANT
(E) EMBATTLED

9 Two three-letter words will go into the brackets to complete two other words. Give both words.

C A (– – –) E T

10 Which gentleman has changed his appearance?

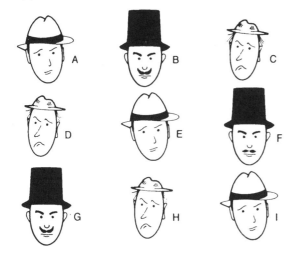

11 What are x and y?

7 8 6 9 5 10 x y

12 Which of these moons are waxing (becoming larger)?

A   B   C   D   E   F

13 Which of the words at the right goes with those at the left?

PASSED
EARTHS
DAD SIMON

(A) BLUSC
(B) ASSET
(C) PALMS
(D) SPARE

14 Which shield is wrong?

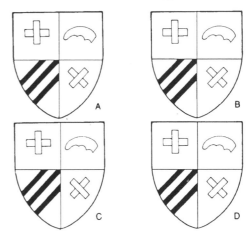

15 Add the difference between the two lowest numbers to the difference between the two highest numbers:

91 13 76 12 7 88 17 84 11
14 87 15 86 16 89 85

NOW CHECK YOUR ANSWERS AND RECORD YOUR SCORE.

1 Which is the odd one out?

(A) CHAPEL
(B) PROBING
(C) SCATTER

2 Assuming that the top two cars are correct, which of those below are wrong?

A

B

C

D

E

3 What are x and y?

1   3   3   6   5   9   7   12   x   y

4 What places are these?

(A) U V S J O
(B) Q B S J T
(C) M P O E P O
(D) C F S M J O

5 What letter completes this word?

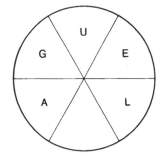

6 Change KNIT into SHOP in four moves, changing one letter at a time.

KNIT
1 – – – –
2 – – – –
3 – – – –
4 SHOP

7 The same three-letter word inside the brackets will complete all these words:

S C (– – –)
B E H (– – –)
H (– – –) A L L
S (– – –) I E R

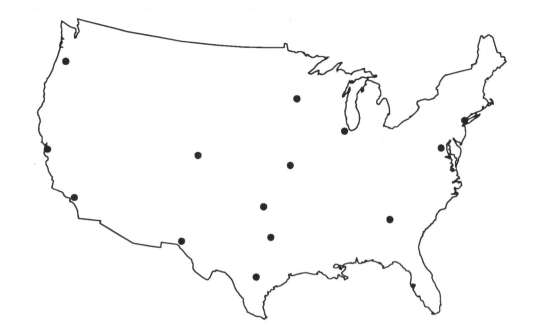

8 The map above shows the places listed below. Using your eyes only, imagine a line joining Dallas to Minneapolis. Now imagine a line going from Washington D.C. to San Francisco. What city will be nearest to the intersection of these lines?

ATLANTA
CHICAGO
DALLAS
DENVER
EL PASO
KANSAS CITY
LOS ANGELES

9 Which is the odd one out?

(A) ARTIST
(B) I START
(C) TRAITS
(D) STAIRS
(E) STRAIT
(F) IT'S TAR

10 Which soccer player is incorrectly dressed?

11 Which of these could NOT be drawn with a continuous unbroken line without crossing another line?

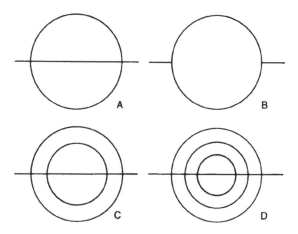

12 Subtract the sum of the three lowest numbers from the sum of the three highest numbers.

11 36 7 38 3 45 39 10 48 37 12 36

13 Two answers are required here.

(A) Can you make sense out of this?
THEM OMEN TOFT RUTH
(B) Can you make sense out of this?
HAL FALO AFIS BET TERT
HAN NOB READ

14 Which word in the second line belongs to the group in the first line?

DOG CAT PIG RABBIT
APE EWE EAGLE ERNE LAMB

15 Group these pictures into four pairs.

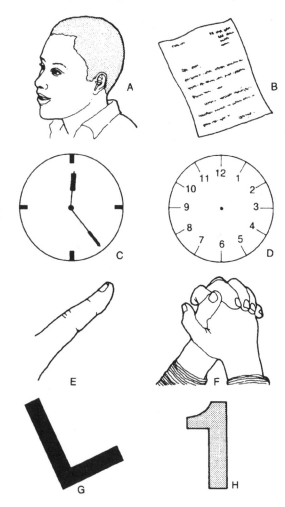

NOW CHECK YOUR ANSWERS AND RECORD YOUR SCORE.

TEST 4

TIME LIMIT: 15 MINUTES

1 Which is the odd one out?

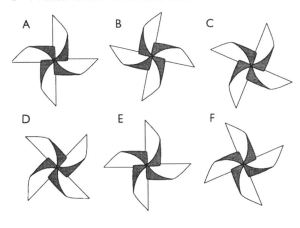

2 What is the last term in this series?

B 2 T G 7 C –

3 What one word can be added to each letter to form the words for which definitions are given?

(A) C		Unfledged
(B) F		Uncultivated
(C) H		Honor as sacred
(D) M		Plant
(E) S		Pale brown
(F) T		Grease
(G) W		Roll about

4 What comes next?

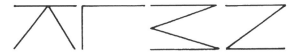

5 What is x?

4 9 x 25

6 Whose face is wrong?

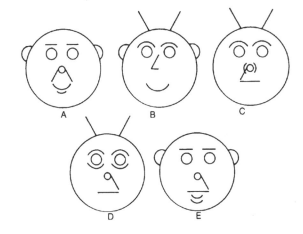

7 What WORD should take the place of x?

W x F S S

8 Give words that will fit each definition.

(A) Part of the body – Coffer
(B) Theater seat – Play for time
(C) Aircraft – Carpenter's tool
(D) Precious stones – Suit
(E) Animal part – Target
(F) Herb – Naïve
(G) Cultivate – Groom
(H) Horny growth – Grain
(I) Dance – Sphere
(J) Game – Metal rod

9 Which one is wrong?

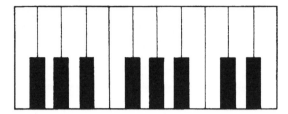

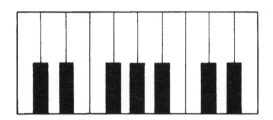

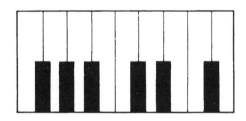

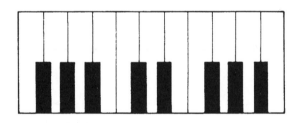

10 What comes next?

208   CIV   52   XXVI   –

11 Which one does not conform with the others?

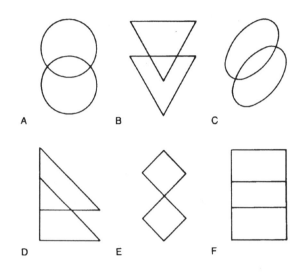

A   B   C

D   E   F

12 Find the words that go into the brackets. Each one must logically follow the previous word and precede the next: e.g. SAFETY (CURTAIN) RAISER.

ELASTIC
(   )
MASTER
(   )
WORK
(   )
WINDOW
(   )
TABLE
(   )
GLASS

13 Which knot is different?

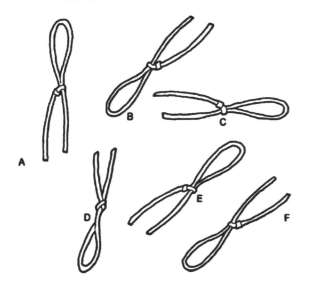

14 What letter completes the word?

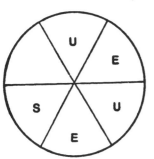

15 Which date does not conform with the others?

(A) 1417 (B) 1533 (C) 1605 (D) 1722
(E) 1812 (F) 1902

NOW CHECK YOUR ANSWERS AND RECORD YOUR SCORE.

1 Pair words in the first column with words in the second column, finishing with ten related pairs.

(A) MIDDLE	(1) COAT
(B) OLYMPIC	(2) FATHER
(C) BULL	(3) GO
(D) TURN	(4) GROUND
(E) OVER	(5) LADDER
(F) UNDER	(6) AROUND
(G) FOR	(7) STILE
(H) OUT	(8) STAND
(I) GRAND	(9) BID
(J) STEP	(10) GAMES

2 Which one is wrong?

(A) $9/4 + 1.75 = 4$

(B) $9/5 + 2.2 = 4$

(C) $6/5 + 2.8 = 4$

(D) $6/4 + 1.5 = 4$

(E) $9/6 + 2.5 = 4$

3 Arrange these zodiac signs in their relative pairs.

(1) ARIES	(A) WATER CARRIER
(2) CANCER	(B) ARCHER
(3) AQUARIUS	(C) CRAB
(4) LIBRA	(D) FISHES
(5) PISCES	(E) RAM
(6) SAGITTARIUS	(F) SCALES

4 Arrange these into five pairs.

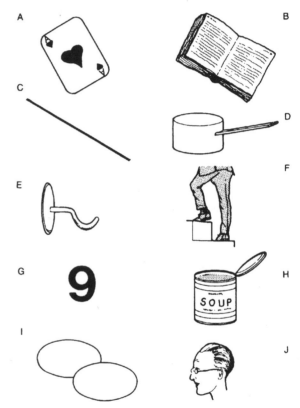

5 Words are often associated in pairs, such as 'ducks and drakes'. Complete these pairs:

(A) CHAPTER and—

(B) —and READY

(C) BAG and—

(D) VIM and—

(E) —and ENDS

(F) CUT and—

(G) HIT and—

(H) —and FURIOUS

(I) —and PARCEL

6 What is x?

1 2 4 8 1 6 3 2 6 x

---

7 WITHOUT REFERRING, whose picture appears on one side of a half dollar coin?

---

8 Multiply the second highest number by the second lowest number and then divide the result by the third lowest number.

10 35 2 32 37 33 9
13 36 12 14 34 3 11

---

9 What is x?

3 6 10 15 x 28

---

10 What comes next?

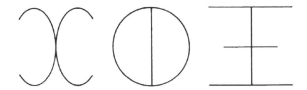

---

11 Which is the odd one out?

(A) TOMATO
(B) CABBAGE
(C) POTATO
(D) LEEK
(E) CARROT

---

12 Which of the circles at the bottom should take the place of No. 2 at the top?

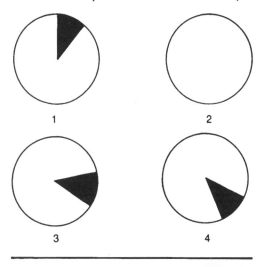

1   2

3   4

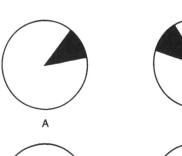

A   B

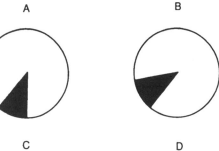

C   D

13 If the two figures at the top are correct, which of those below are wrong?

A   B

 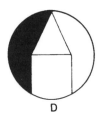

C   D

E   F

14 Two different letters placed in the empty segment will form two different words. Give both letters.

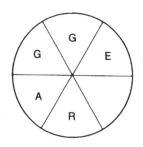

15 Which one is wrong?

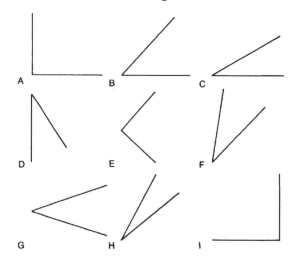

NOW CHECK YOUR ANSWERS AND
RECORD YOUR SCORE.

I What letter will complete this word?

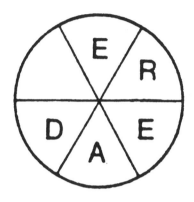

2 Which one of these figures is wrong?

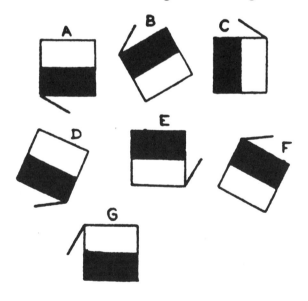

3 Add the two highest numbers and take away the sum of the three lowest numbers.

16 13 9 11 23 19 5 14 12 15 18 17

4 If 63542 equals 52634, what is: BCDEF?

5 Join these syllables in pairs to make ten words:

REC LET LOON SORE AD BAL TOM FUR ER ORD BRE TAB OR CAT EYE HER BOY SA OUT LE

6 Arrange these into four pairs:

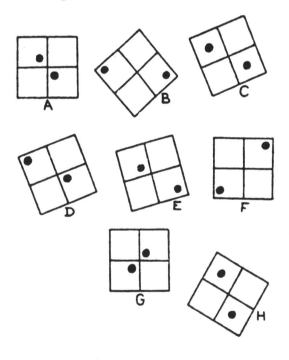

7 What are the last two terms in this series?

Z 13Y 14W 16T 19 - -

8 Which is the odd one out?

(A) LIRA (B) MARKS (C) DRACHMAE (D) RAND
(E) FRANCS

9 Which is the odd one out?

(A) YLAP (B) APREO (C) VEERU (D) RENCOCT
(E) SHECS

10 Which of these is wrong?

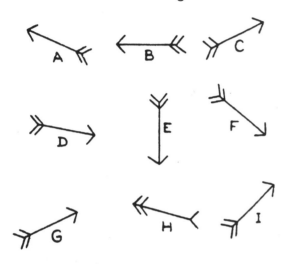

11 Which date does not conform with the others?

(A) 1584 (B) 1692 (C) 1729 (D) 1809 (E) 1980

12 Which is the odd one out?

(A) ELIGIBLE (B) SHEEPISH (C) DELIGHTED
(D) FOOLPROOF (E) GNASHING

13 Arrange these words in alphabetical order:

(A) ABRACADABRA (B) ABOUT (C) ABBEY
(D) ABUNDANCE (E) ABACUS (F) ABOULIA (G)
ABBOT

14 Who has changed his expression?

15 Which of these shields are identical?

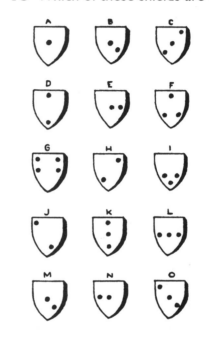

NOW CHECK YOUR ANSWERS AND RECORD YOUR SCORE.

TEST 7

TIME LIMIT: 35 MINUTES

1 What goes into the empty brackets?

144 (3625) 125 96 (1618) 126 112 ( ) 144

2 Fill in the brackets. The word in each set of brackets must logically follow the previous word and precede the following word, e.g., library (BOOK) mark.

BULL
( )
HOUSE
( )
YARD
( )
BATH
( )
FALL
( )
SIDE
( )
WAY

3 Using your eye only, which is the missing brick?

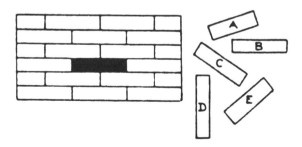

4 Which is the odd one out?

5 Arrange these strange-looking insects into four pairs:

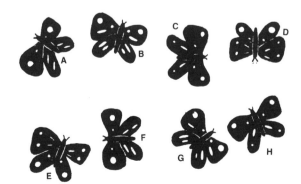

6 What is X?

J M M J S N X

---

7 Which one is wrong?

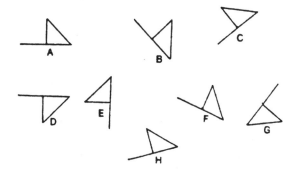

---

8 Arrange the labels into four pairs:

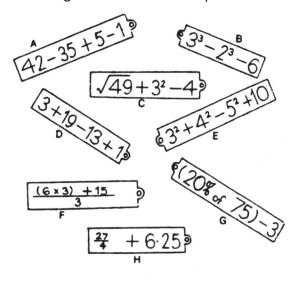

---

9 What is X?

---

10 Complete these words, for which definitions are given

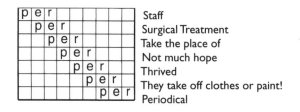

Staff
Surgical Treatment
Take the place of
Not much hope
Thrived
They take off clothes or paint!
Periodical

---

11 Arrange these patterns into four pairs.

---

12 Which of these does not belong?

4 18 16 8 24

13 Change RAIN into SNOW in three moves, changing TWO letters at a time.

14 Which is the odd one out?

(A) PROVERBS (B) RUTH (C) EZEKIEL
(D) CORINTHIANS (E) NUMBERS (F) PSALMS

15 Assuming that the top two stars are correct, which of those below are wrong?

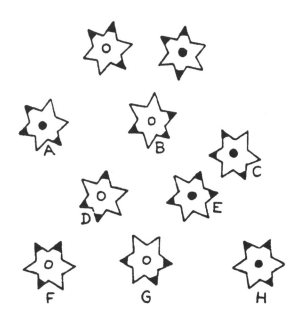

NOW CHECK YOUR ANSWERS AND RECORD YOUR SCORE.

TEST 8

TIME LIMIT: 45 MINUTES

1 What are X and Y?

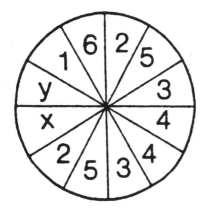

2 Which is the odd one out?

(A) CABBAGE (B) HAPPY (C) FELLOW
(D) KURSAAL (E) GLIMMER

3 Complete the words to fit the definitions.
The number of missing letters is indicated by
dashes.

HAPPEN	– – – – – – IRE
DRESS	– – IRE
PLOT	– – – – – IRE
DIE	– – – – IRE
WHOLE	– – – IRE
DOMINION	– – – IRE
BOG	– – – – – IRE
LAMPOON	– – – IRE
ARBITRATOR	– – – IRE

4
If is superimposed on

which of the OUTLINES below will result?

5 Which column does not conform?

A	B	C	D	E	F
17	14	22	31	29	33
9	13	15	22	19	8
13	11	17	17	31	19
24	7	2	13	5	20
2	29	8	4	2	17
10	6	21	3	10	3

6 If the figure below were held in front of a mirror and the mirror turned upside-down, which of the other figures would be reflected?

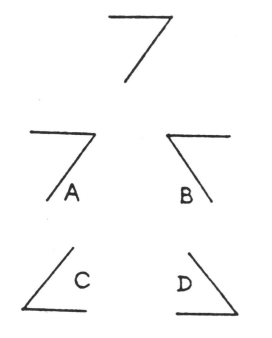

7 Which is the odd one out?

(A) STARLING
(B) PARTRIDGE
(C) GROUSE
(D) BLUETIT
(E) CUCKOO-PINT
(F) LARK
(G) NIGHTINGALE

8 Which row is wrong?

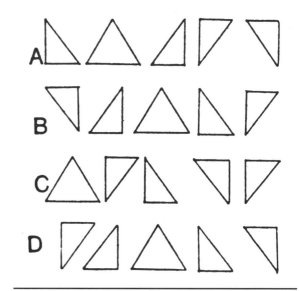

9 What is two days after the day after the day before yesterday?

10 Which is the odd word out?

(A) MEDICAL
(B) BATTLE
(C) ARTICLE
(D) BALLET
(E) RECITAL
(F) CLAIMED
(G) TABLET

11 Give words described by these definitions. Each word must contain AND.

(A) Evergreen shrub
(B) Lizard-like animal
(C) Stray
(D) Footwear
(E) Baton
(F) Part of Scotland
(G) Sweets
(H) Have many love affairs
(I) Strainer

12 Which trellis is wrong?

13 If 3(76) equals 212 and 4(320) equals 125 what is 5(6100)?

14 Without turning the page upside down, which of these numbers will not read the same when turned upside-down?

A 81698

B 81818

C 189981

D 116911

E 196961

15 One of these words is spelled incorrectly. Which one?

(A) RECEIVE
(B) IMMANENT
(C) FASCIA
(D) DESSICATED
(E) BUDGERIGAR
(F) SCHISM
(G) PNEUMONIA
(H) NASCENT
(I) LEMUR
(J) CHEETAH

NOW CHECK YOUR ANSWERS AND RECORD YOUR SCORE.

1 Which of the symbols at the bottom should take the place of X?

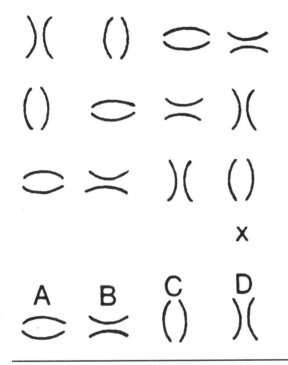

2 What is X?

2 1 8 5 9
3 7 2 6 2
4 2 1 1 X

3 Supply the missing letter. (Proper nouns not allowed)

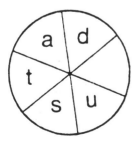

4 Which is the odd one out?

(A) SHORE (B) KEPI (C) TUTOR (D) ASSB

5 Which letter does not conform with the others?

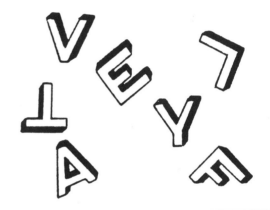

6 What WORD is represented by X?

31 31 X 31

7 Which is the odd one out?

(A) TESTAMENT   (D) GRAVAMEN
(B) PROMINENCE   (E) FLAMENCO
(C) FILAMENT   (F) STAMENS

8 Give words to fit these definitions. Each word must contain a part of the body:

(A) Apparatus for applying mechanical power
(B) Fast time for a musician
(C) Gardener's means of transport
(D) Uttering of speech
(E) Nautical pal
(F) Security device

9 Arrange these into six pairs:

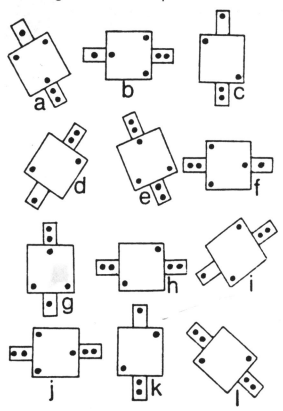

10 What is X?

3 6 10 15 X 28

11 Give words to fit these definitions. Each word must start with the last two letters of the previous word.

(A) STAR
(B) FISH
(C) END OF THE LINE
(D) CUSTOMARY PRACTICE
(E) ARMY OFFICER
(F) DIVORCE ALLOWANCE
(G) SYNTHETIC FIBER
(H) ATTACK
(I) WORD EXPERT
(J) THOROUGHFARE

12 Which are the weak links?

13 What four letter word placed inside the brackets will complete all of these words?

A(– – – –)NT   SUB(– – – –)   (– – – –)RICK

14 What are X & Y?

7 8 6 9 5 10 X Y 3 12

15 Arrange these shapes in order according to the number of sides, starting with the one with the least number:

(A) OCTAGON
(B) HEXAGON
(C) PENTAGON
(D) DECAGON
(E) TETRAGON
(F) NONAGON
(G) HEPTAGON

NOW CHECK YOUR ANSWERS AND RECORD YOUR SCORE.

TEST 1 ANSWERS

1 d. So that each corner sub-square of each of the four main sections has a line missing.

2 e. There are two black arms—one moves through 90 degrees each time and the other through 45 degrees. The dotted line never moves but is covered by the black arms when they coincide with its position.

3 Nil. If three are correct then four must be.

4 2/1. The number of pictures on the card does not affect the odds.

5 Across: 2. Man, 4. Begot, 6. Paraded, 8. Hare, 9. Elan, 11. Role, 12. Lies, 14. Beta, 15. Reed, 16. Deck, 18. Side, 19. Leaf, 21. Apes, 22. Sleeves, 24. Elbow, 25. Low.

Down: 1. Saga, 2. Mere, 3. Node, 4. Bare, 5. Tell, 6. Palaces, 7. Dairies, 8. Hotel, 10. Needs, 11. Red, 13. See, 17. Kale, 18. Spew, 20. Fell, 21. Avow, 23. Ebon.

6 1. Paled, 2. Azure, 3. Lucre, 4. Erred, 5. Deeds, 6. Trade, 7. Riled, 8. Alibi, 9. Debit, 10. Edits, 11. State, 12. Tutor, 13. Atone, 14. Tonic, 15. Erect, 16. Masse, 17. Aches, 18. Shops, 19. Sepia, 20. Essay, 21. Tramp, 22. Racer, 23. Acute, 24. Metes, 25. Press.

7 How often have I said to you that when you have eliminated the impossible, whatever remains, however improbable, must be the truth?

[Conan] Doyle

Message keyed (ELMNTARYDWSO):

Elementary, my dear Watson.

8 It is known to many that we need solitude to find ourselves. Perhaps it is not so well known that we need solitude to find our fellows. Even the Savior is described as reaching mankind through the wilderness.

Havelock Ellis

Message keyed (HIDEANSK): Hide and Seek.

9 It is pi to nine decimal places: 3.141592654.

10 -40 degrees Centigrade is the same as -40 degrees Fahrenheit.

11 17: All numbers, when written out, contain only "E" vowels.

12 At some time during the calculation you will be multiplying by (x-x), which equals 0, therefore the product will be 0.

13 He puts down four dimes and two nickels. If he had wanted Budweiser he would have put down four dimes and one nickel.

14 He had already sugared the tea. When the waiter returned with the supposedly fresh cup, he sugared it again and knew it was the original tea as soon as he took the first sip.

15 (a) COUPLES FLIRTING; **(b)** MUTTERING THROUGH MOUSTACHE.

16 (a) Racoon, **(b)** Leopard, **(c)** Terrier, **(d)** Lioness, **(e)** Samoyed, **(f)** Spaniel, **(g)** Carthorse, **(h)** African lion.

17 (a) They contain their square root, i.e., 3**600**, 5**776**; 2**500** is the other four-figure number sharing this feature.

(b) Their two halves added together equal their square root, i.e., 2025 (20 + 25 = 45) and $45^2 = 2025$. The other four-figure number sharing this feature is 3025.

18 2. The initial letters of the others spell out musical instruments: flute, harp, tuba.

19 e. It is the only one where the dot is inside the circle.

20 Crypt, Rhythm, Tryst, Hymn, Nymph.

21 (a) Hell, **(b)** Soon, **(c)** Fresh, **(d)** Effete, **(e)** Push, **(f)** Sever, **(g)** Alone, **(h)** Adored, **(i)** Recite, **(j)** Elegant, **(k)** Recreant, **(l)** Doyen, **(m)** Loiter, **(n)** New.

22 Pam has twins aged three and triplets aged one, i.e., $3 \times 3 \times 1 \times 1 \times 1 = 3 + 3 + 1 + 1 + 1$. Fran has triplets aged two and twins aged one, i.e., $2 \times 2 \times 2 \times 1 \times 1 = 2 + 2 + 2 + 1 + 1$.

23 $9 + 8 + 7 + 6 - 5 - 4 - 3 + 2 - 1 = 0$

24 Roy on Tuesday, Terry on Wednesday. The names appear in alphabetical order, as do the days of the week.

25 It was raining: "Rain" is an anagram of Iran; "plane" is an anagram of Nepal; "chain" is an anagram of China.

26 (g) SX. Each square contains the first and last letters of the numbers one to nine positioned in such a way so as to form a magic square where each horizontal, vertical, and corner-to-corner line totals 15.

27 (a) Whimsy, **(b)** Slapstick, **(c)** Banter, **(d)** Caricature, **(e)** Buffoonery, **(f)** Burlesque, **(g)** Jocularity, **(h)** Spoof, **(i)** Badinage, **(j)** Satire, **(k)** Farce, **(l)** Cartoon, **(m)** Hoax, **(n)** Comedy.

1 (1) (E); (2) (F); (3) (I); (4) (A); (5) (G); (6) (H); (7) (C); (8) (D); (9) (B) **(SCORE 1 IF ALL CORRECT; SCORE ½ POINT IF 8 ARE CORRECT).**
TENNIS can pair only with MATCH, therefore SAFETY must pair with LOCK. SEE can pair only with SAW, therefore SHOP must pair with WORK. TOY can pair only with STORE, so WORK must pair with BENCH. BAND must go with AGE (SAW has already been used). That leaves IRON and HOUSE in the first column and CLAD and HOLD in the second, which means that HOUSE must pair with HOLD and IRON with CLAD.

2 C **(SCORE 1 POINT).**
The middle scrolls do not conform with the others.

3 S 19 **(SCORE 1 POINT IF BOTH ARE CORRECT).**
There are two separate series. The letters advance missing the first two (A to D), then three (D to H) and so on. After M there must be five missing letters, bringing us to S. The numbers advance in the same way.

4 **(SCORE 1 POINT IF ALL ARE CORRECT).**
(A) NORMAN   (B) IRIS   (C) ANNE
(D) RICHARD
In (A) the letters have been increased by one place in the alphabet, in (B) by two places, in (C) by three places and in (D) by four places.

5 (D) **(SCORE 1 POINT).**
RAND is the unit currency in South Africa. All the others are slang terms for currency:
(A) GRAND – 1,000 dollars
(B) TEN-SPOT – 10 dollars
(C) BUCK – dollar
(D) C-NOTE – 100 dollars
(E) BEN FRANKLIN – 100 dollars
(F) CLAM – dollar
(G) GREENBACK – dollar
(I) FIVER – 5 dollars

6 F **(SCORE 1 POINT).**
Both scrolls are turned the same way; in all the others one is turned inwards and the other outwards.

7 (D) **(SCORE 1 POINT).**
Since 1764 was a leap year, there were 29 days in February, so it would be Saturday, March 10 not March 11.

8 (A) **(SCORE 1 POINT).**
All the other words contain BAT. CONSTABLE contains those letters in reverse order.

9 BIN and BAR **(SCORE 1 POINT IF BOTH ARE CORRECT).**
The words are CABINET and CABARET.

10 F **(SCORE 1 POINT).**
His mustache differs from B and G.

11 x is 4; y is 11 **(SCORE 1 POINT IF BOTH ARE CORRECT).**
There are two alternate series.
One is: 7   6   5   4
The other is: 8   9   10   11

12 A, B and E **(SCORE 1 POINT IF ALL ARE CORRECT).**
With regard to the shape of the moon, D comes before C: when the moon is in the shape of D it is waxing and when in the shape of C it is waning (diminishing in size).

13 (A) **(SCORE 1 POINT).**
This is an anagram of CLUBS, and the three on top are anagrams of the other suits:
PASSED – SPADES; EARTHS – HEARTS;
DAD SIMON – DIAMONDS

14 C **(SCORE 1 POINT).**
The cross in the bottom right quarter is different from those in the other shields.

15 6 **(SCORE 1 POINT).**

NOTES

1, 4, 7 and 13 caused the most difficulty or took the longest time to solve. Most points were lost on 4 and 13.
However, on the whole the problems in this test were not too difficult. They were deliberately intended to introduce you gently to the types of problems you will encounter later, which will become progressively more difficult.

1 (B) **(SCORE 1 POINT)**.
This word contains a bird – ROBIN. All the others contain animals:
(A) APE (C) CAT (D) LION (E) BEAR
(F) HARE

2 C and F **(SCORE 1 POINT IF BOTH ARE CORRECT)**.

3 x is 9; y is 15 **(SCORE 1 POINT IF BOTH ARE CORRECT)**.
There are two separate series. Starting with the first number and taking the others alternately:
1 3 5 7 9
Starting with the second number and proceeding the same way:
3 6 9 12 15

4 **(SCORE 1 POINT IF ALL ARE CORRECT)**.
(A) TURIN (B) PARIS (C) LONDON
(D) BERLIN
Each letter is reduced by one in the alphabet.

5 E **(SCORE 1 POINT)**.
The word is LEAGUE.

6 KNIT; 1 SNIT; 2 SNIP; 3 SHIP; 4 SHOP **(SCORE 1 POINT)**.
(You may have used other words, but you still score one point provided they are actual words.)

7 OLD **(SCORE 1 POINT)**.
The words are: SCOLD; BEHOLD; HOLDALL; SOLDIER.

8 KANSAS CITY **(SCORE 1 POINT)**.

9 (D) **(SCORE 1 POINT)**.
All the others are anagrams of ARTIST.

10 E **(SCORE 1 POINT)**.
Soccer players in black short wear black socks; those in white shorts wear white socks. E is wearing black shorts and white socks.

11 B **(SCORE 1 POINT)**.
As can be seen below, all the others can be drawn with a continuous unbroken line:

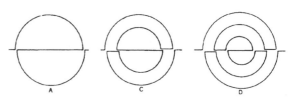

12 112 **(SCORE 1 POINT)**.

13 **(SCORE 1 POINT IF BOTH ARE CORRECT.)**
(A) THE MOMENT OF TRUTH
(B) HALF A LOAF IS BETTER THAN NO BREAD

14 LAMB **(SCORE 1 POINT)**.
All the words in the first line begin and end with a consonant. In the second line all the words begin and end with a vowel—except LAMB.

15 A D; B G; C F; E H **(SCORE 1 POINT IF ALL CORRECT)**.
The pairs are the same words with different connotations:
FACE (human) – clock FACE
LETTER (communication) – LETTER (alphabet)
HANDS (clock) – HANDS (human)
DIGIT (human) – DIGIT (numerical)

NOTES

None of the problems should have held you up for very long, as little writing was involved.
4 and 8 caused the longest delay. In 2 'are wrong' told you that more than one was wrong, whereas in 10 'is incorrect' told you that only one was wrong.
The best clue in 7 was provided by
B E H (– – –), since the only six-letter words which begin with these letters are: BEHALF, BEHAVE, BEHEAD, BEHELD, BEHEST, BEHIND, BEHOLD, BEHOOF and BEHOVE. Obviously, ALF, AVE, EAD, ELD, EST, IND, OOF and OVE will not fit the other words. The only one that is common to all is OLD.

1 B **(SCORE 1 POINT).**

2 3 **(SCORE 1 POINT).**
The numbers following the letters correspond with the position in the alphabet of the letters.

3 ALLOW **(SCORE 1 POINT).**
The words are: (A) CALLOW; (B) FALLOW;
(C) HALLOW; (D) MALLOW; (E) SALLOW;
(F) TALLOW; (G) WALLOW

4 O **(SCORE 1 POINT).**
The letters K L M N have been turned on their sides. O is the next letter.

5 16 **(SCORE 1 POINT).**
4 is the square of 2; 9 is the square of 3; 25 is the square of 5; x must be the square of 4 (16).

6 B **(SCORE 1 POINT).**
The face in B is composed of three circles, four straight lines and five curves. All the other faces have four circles, four straight lines and four curves.

7 THURSDAY **(SCORE 1 POINT).**
Obviously they are the days of the week:
W   Wednesday
T   Thursday
F   Friday
S   Saturday
S   Sunday
(Note: T alone is not acceptable, as the question asks what WORD should take the place of x.)

8 **(SCORE 1 POINT IF ALL CORRECT; ½ IF 8 OR 9.)**
(A) CHEST; (B) STALL; (C) PLANE;
(D) DIAMONDS; (E) BULLSEYE; (F) SIMPLE
(G) HUSBAND; (H) CORN; (I) BALL; (J) POKER

9 A **(SCORE 1 POINT).**
These are the keys of a piano. It is not possible to have two groups of three black keys next to each other.

10 13 **(SCORE 1 POINT).**
Change the Roman numerals into modern numbers:
208   104   52   26
Each one is half the previous number. Therefore the next number is 13, expressed in modern numerals to conform with the established pattern.

11 E **(SCORE 1 POINT).**
In all the others identical shapes overlap:
(A) two circles
(B) two equilateral triangles
(C) two ovals
(D) two right-angled triangles
(F) two squares
In E there are two diamonds which do not overlap.

12 **(SCORE 1 POINT IF ALL ARE CORRECT.)**
BAND
PIECE
SHOP
DRESSING
WINE

13 D **(SCORE 1 POINT).**

14 Q **(SCORE 1 POINT).**
The word is QUEUES.

15 (A) **(SCORE 1 POINT).**
With the exception of the digits in (A), which add up to 13, the digits in all the other dates add up to 12

TEST 5 ANSWERS

1 (A) (4); (B) (10); (C) (6); (D) (7); (E) (1); (F) (8); (G) (3); (H) (9); (I) (2); (J) (5)
(SCORE 1 POINT IF ALL ARE CORRECT; ½ IF 8 OR 9.)

2 (D) **(SCORE 1 POINT)**.
(D) equals 3; all the others equal 4.

3 (SCORE 1 POINT IF ALL ARE CORRECT).
(1) (E); (2) (C); (3) (A); (4) (F); (5) (D); (6) (B)

4 (SCORE 1 POINT IF ALL ARE CORRECT.)
Rhyming pairs:

A	(ACE)	J	(FACE)
B	(BOOK)	E	(HOOK)
C	(LINE)	G	(NINE)
D	(PAN)	H	(CAN)
F	(LEGS)	I	(EGGS)

5 (SCORE 1 POINT IF ALL ARE CORRECT; ½ IF 7 OR 8.)
(A) VERSE; (B) ROUGH; (C) BAGGAGE; (D) VIM; (E) ODDS; (F) PASTE; (G) RUN; (H) FAST; (I) PART;

6 4 **(SCORE 1 POINT)**.
The series is incorrectly spaced. When corrected it reads:
1 2 4 8 16 32 64

7 John F. Kennedy **(SCORE 1 POINT)**.

8 12 **(SCORE 1 POINT)**.

9 21 **(SCORE 1 POINT)**.
The numbers increase by 3, 4, 5, 6 and 7.

10 (SCORE 1 POINT).
The letters are C, D and E. In each case they are paired and joined together, first reversed and then printed correctly. The next letter is F, arranged in the same way.

11 (A) **(SCORE 1 POINT)**.
TOMATO is a fruit. All the others are vegetables.

12 A **(SCORE 1 POINT)**.
The black section rotates clockwise 40° at a time.

13 C, D, E **(SCORE 1 POINT IF ALL ARE CORRECT)**.

14 D and B **(SCORE 1 POINT IF BOTH ARE CORRECT)**.
The words are RAGGED and BEGGAR.

15 G **(SCORE 1 POINT)**.
The angle is 60°. The others are 90°, 45° or 30°.

NOTES

There were no great difficulties in this test.
14 gave some trouble: although RAGGED stood out fairly prominently, BEGGAR was not so obvious.

ELEMENTARY LEVEL **44** TEST 5 ANSWERS

TEST 6 ANSWERS

1 (H) **(SCORE 1 POINT)**
The word is ADHERE

2 (A) **(SCORE 1 POINT)**
When the diagonal line from the base-line of the square inclines to the right, as in C, E, and G, the right half of the square is black. When it inclines to the left, as in B, D, and F, the bottom half of the square is black. In A, the right half of the square should be black.

3 17 **(SCORE 1 POINT)**

4 DCFBE **(SCORE 1 POINT)**

5 **(SCORE 1 POINT IF ALL ARE CORRECT; 1/2 POINT IF 8 ARE CORRECT)**

REC-ORD	EYE-SORE
CAT-ER	OUT-LET
TOM-BOY	SA-LOON
TAB-LE	BRE-AD
HER-BAL	FUR-OR

6 AG BF CH DE
(SCORE 1 POINT IF ALL CORRECT)

7 P 23 **(SCORE 1 POINT IF BOTH ARE CORRECT)**. Two separate series. Letters descend alphabetically, first to the next letter, then skipping one, then two, and so on. The numbers rise in the same way.

8 (B) **(SCORE 1 POINT)**.
All the currencies contain the letters RA in that order. In MARKS these letters are reversed.

9 (E) **(SCORE 1 POINT)**.
An anagram of CHESS. All the others are anagrams of types of entertainment:
(A) PLAY   (C) REVUE
(B) OPERA   (D) CONCERT

10 (H) **(SCORE 1 POINT)**.
The point has two barbs instead of one, and one set of tail feathers instead of two.

11 (C) **(SCORE 1 POINT)**
The digits add up to 19. In all the others they add up to 18.

12 (B) **(SCORE 1 POINT)**
It starts and ends with the same two letters. All the others start and end with the same two letters reversed.

13 (E) (C) (G) (F) (B) (A) (D) **(SCORE 1 POINT)**.

14 (J) **(SCORE 1 POINT)**.
The mouth should be the same as in B and H.

15 B and M
(SCORE 1 POINT)

NOTES

Although all of the tests in this book are graded according to difficulty, in any one section some problems are more difficult (or easier) than others. The dividing line is slim between a difficult problem in one section and an easy one in the next. In the end, however, the final count of "easy" and "difficult" problems is immaterial, because the ultimate ratings are based on all the problems collectively. In imposing time limits, two factors have been considered: 1. The fact that some problems require fairly lengthy written answers (as opposed to simply writing a number or a letter); 2. Some people write faster than others. Accordingly, where written answers are involved, not only has a longer time been allowed, but time has been taken from that of comparatively slow writers. Number 5 in the previous test took our volunteers longer— because of the amount of writing involved, and because it calls for a great deal of "trial and error" deduction. Success depends largely on making a lucky guess among alternatives. Other problems which caused delay in answering—or failure to answer correctly—were 8 and 12, each calling for deductions beyond the obvious. In the case of 8, the fact that one currency is non-European would not have been as strong an answer as the one given in the answer section.

TEST 7 ANSWERS

1 1416 **(SCORE 1 POINT)** In the first example, divide the left-hand number by 4 and the right-hand number by 5. In the second example, divide the left-hand number by 6 and the right-hand number by 7. Therefore, in the third line, divide the left-hand number by 8(14) and the right-hand number by 9(16).

2 DOG-BOAT-BIRD-WATER-OUT-WALK **(SCORE 1 POINT IF ALL ARE CORRECT)**

3 C **(SCORE 1 POINT)**

4 F **(SCORE 1 POINT)**

5 AF BG CH DE **(SCORE 1 POINT)**

6 J **(SCORE 1 POINT)** The initials are the months of the year. The sequence is every two months; January, March, May, etc. the answer is J for January.

7 D **(SCORE 1 POINT)**. The triangle should be on the right-hand side of the base-line.

8 AF BH CG DE **(SCORE 1 POINT)**.
A and F each equal 11.
B and H each equal 13.
C and G each equal 12.
D and E each equal 10.

9 B **(SCORE 1 POINT)**.

In each section, the letters in the outer ring combine with those in the inner ring to form a word in conjunction with LAND which is common to all the words:

IS	LAND	ER
G	LAND	ULAR
OUT	LAND	ISH
UP	LAND	S
S	LAND	ER
GAR	LAND	S
B	LAND	ISHMENT (X IS B)

10 **(SCORE 1 POINT IF ALL ARE CORRECT; SCORE ½ POINT IF 6 ARE CORRECT.)**.

PERSONNEL	PROSPERED
OPERATION	STRIPPERS
SUPERCEDE	NEWSPAPER
DESPERATE	

11 AE BD CG FH **(SCORE 1 POINT)**

12 18 **(SCORE 1 POINT)**
All the others are divisible by 4.

13 **(SCORE 1 POINT FOR THE FOLLOWING, OR FOR OTHER WORDS, PROVIDED THEY ARE REAL WORDS AND FULFILL THE REQUIREMENT OF CHANGING TWO LETTERS AT A TIME):**

	R A I N
1	S A I L
2	S N I P
3	S N O W

14 D **(SCORE 1 POINT)**. CORINTHIANS is in the New Testament; all the others are in the Old Testament.

15 F and H **(SCORE 1 POINT IF BOTH ARE CORRECT)**

NOTES

Most time was lost by volunteers on 1, 2, 8, and 13. Few were able to solve 1 within the time limit, yet one person arrived at the answer almost immediately. He was a mathematics teacher at a high school! The relationship between the numbers outside the brackets and those inside struck him instantly, substantiating the fact that one person will excel in a subject for which a special aptitude is an advantage, whereas another will be stumped by it. Obviously, 8 took some time to solve, as each of the mathematical problems had to be solved individually. In 13, the necessity for changing TWO letters at a time created considerable confusion.

TEST 8 ANSWERS

1 X is 6; Y is 1 **(SCORE 1 POINT IF BOTH ARE CORRECT)**. Starting at the number 1 and moving to alternate segments clockwise:
1 2 3 4 5 6
Starting at number 6 and moving the same way:
6 5 4 3 2 1

2 D **(SCORE 1 POINT)** In KURSAAL there are two identical adjacent vowels. In all of the other words there are two identical adjacent consonants.

3 **(SCORE 1 POINT IF ALL ARE CORRECT; ½ IF 7 OR 8 ARE CORRECT.)**

TRANSPIRE	EMPIRE
ATTIRE	QUAGMIRE
CONSPIRE	SATIRE
EXPIRE	UMPIRE
ENTIRE	

4 B **(SCORE 1 POINT)**

5 E **(SCORE 1 POINT)**
Adding up each column:

Column A= 75	Column D= 90
Column B= 80	Column E= 96
Column C= 85	Column F= 100

6 B **(SCORE 1 POINT)**
The fact that the MIRROR (not the figure!) is held upside-down will make no difference to the reflection.

7 E (score 1 point).
CUCKOO-PINT is a flower—the more commonly known arum or wale-robin. All the others are birds.

8 C **(SCORE 1 POINT)**.
Except for C, each row contains 1 equilateral triangle, 2 right-angled triangles with the base at the bottom and 2 with the base at the top. In C there are three right-angled triangles with the base at the top and only one with the base at the bottom.

9 Tomorrow **(SCORE 1 POINT)**.
The day before yesterday was two days ago; the day after yesterday; two days after that (yesterday) is TOMORROW

10 D **(SCORE 1 POINT)**.
Apart from this, the words are paired in anagrams:
(A) MEDICAL with (F) CLAIMED
(B) BATTLE with (G) TABLET
(C) ARTICLE with (E) RECITAL.
No word shown forms an anagram with BALLET.

11 **(SCORE 1 POINT IF ALL ARE CORRECT; ½ POINT IF 8 OR 9 ARE CORRECT)**

(A) OLEANDER	(F) HIGHLANDS or LOWLANDS
(B) SALAMANDER	(G) CANDY
(C) WANDER	(H) PHILANDER
(D) SANDAL	(I) SQUANDER
(E) WAND	(J) COLANDER

12 E **(SCORE 1 POINT)**
The diagonal slat from top left to bottom right should pass under the other slats.

13 3020 **(SCORE 1 POINT)**.
The first two digits on the right side of the brackets are divided by the digits on the left to give the first digit inside the brackets. The remaining number on the right of the brackets is multiplied by the digit on the left side of the brackets to give the remaining number inside the brackets.

14 C **(SCORE 1 POINT)**.

15 D **(SCORE 1 POINT)**
This should be spelled DESICCATED.

NOTES

Questions 3 and 11 called for a fair amount of writing, which is allowed for in the time limit. A few volunteers were stumped by 6, jumping at that appeared to be the obvious, but overlooking the vital fact that the reversal of the mirror makes no difference to the reflection. Many lost points on 7 and 11; in the latter, (A), (B), (H), and (J) caused the most trouble. In 15, the fairly well-recognized general weakness in spelling was revealed. Some volunteers quickly chose IMMANENT as the mis-spelled word—mistaking it for IMMINENT—which is an entirely different word. Remarkably, two chefs failed to spot that DESICCATED was spelled incorrectly!

1 A **(SCORE 1 POINT)**
In each row, the first symbol is the same as the second in the previous row, and the other symbols continue in the same order.

2 2 **(SCORE 1 POINT)**
The first column totals 10. This pattern continues, so the final column should total 13, by the addition of 2.

3 J **(SCORE 1 POINT)**
The word is ADJUST. (Datsun is not allowed)

4 A **(SCORE 1 POINT)**
An anagram of HORSE. All the others are anagrams of fish:
(B) PIKE
(C) TROUT
(D) BASS

5 L **(SCORE 1 POINT)**
The block (the black portion) should be on the right of the letter.

6 SEPTEMBER **(SCORE 1 POINT IF ALL CORRECT)** These are the numbers of days in the months. September is the only month which has two 31-day months before it and one after it.

7 B **(SCORE 1 POINT).**
All of the other words contain AMEN

8 B **(SCORE 1 POINT IF ALL ARE CORRECT; ½ POINT IF 5 ARE CORRECT)**
(A) maCHINe
(B) alLEGro
(C) wHEELbarrow
(D) deLIVERy
(E) sHIPmate
(F) alARM

9 ag ci bf dk ej hl **(SCORE 1 POINT).**

10 21 **(SCORE 1 POINT).**
The numbers increase by 3, 4, 5, 6 and 7.

11 **(SCORE 1 POINT IF ALL ARE CORRECT; ½ POINT IF 8 OR 9 ARE CORRECT.)**
asterISK
SKaTE
TErminUS
USaGE
GEnerAL
ALimoNY
NYlON
ONsET
ETymologiST
STreet

12 G and H **(SCORE 1 POINT)**

13 LIME **(SCORE 1 POINT)**
The words are: aliment sublime limerick

14 X is 4; Y is 11 **(SCORE 1 POINT IF BOTH ARE CORRECT).**
Two alternate series
Starting with the first number: 7 6 5 4 3
Starting with the second number: 8 9 10 11 12

15 **(SCORE 1 POINT IF ALL ARE CORRECT; ½ POINT IF 6 ARE CORRECT.)**
(E) TETRAGON—4 SIDES
(C) PENTAGON—5 SIDES
(B) HEXAGON—6 SIDES
(G) HEPTAGON—7 SIDES
(A) OCTAGON—8 SIDES
(F) NONAGON—9 SIDES
(D) DECAGON—10 SIDES

NOTES

Two of the problems—8 and 11—require fairly long written answers (allowed for in the time limit). The volunteers experienced most difficulty with 8, 11, and 15.

CHALLENGING LEVEL

1 LOGIC

Find the next figure:

(1)   (2)   (3)   (4)   (5)

Choose from:

(a)   (b)   (c)   (d)

2 TROMINOES

Consider the three trominoes below:

Now choose one of the following to accompany the above:

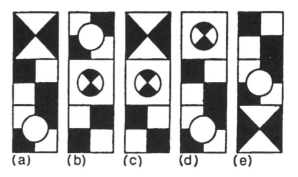
(a)   (b)   (c)   (d)   (e)

3 ADVANCED MATRIX

Look along the line horizontally, and then down each line vertically, to find what, logically, should be the missing square.

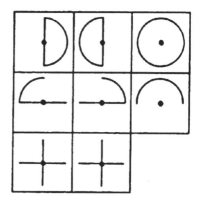

Choose from:

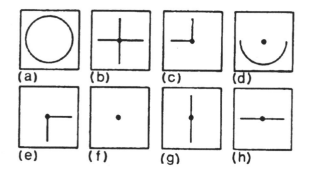

4 HEADS AND TAILS

A friend of yours is tossing a coin and you are betting him on the outcome. You bet on heads every time. Your unit stake is $1 per toss. You begin by betting $1 on the first toss. If you win, you again place $1 on the second toss but if you lose you double the stake to $2, then $4, and continue to double after every loss. After every win you revert to the $1 stake. After 100 tosses of the coin, heads has come down 59 times. How much profit have you made, assuming that the 100th toss was heads?

5 PROBABILITY PARADOX

Four balls are placed in a hat. One is yellow, one is blue and the other two are red. The hat is shaken and someone draws two balls from the hat. He looks at the two balls and announces that one of them is red. What are the chances that the other ball he has drawn out is also red?

6 SNOOKER

The game of snooker is played with 15 red balls, a black, a pink, a blue, a brown, a green, a yellow, and a white ball, which is the cue ball. Apart from the reds, which form a triangle at the top of the table, and the white, each of the remaining six colored balls must be placed on its own spot on the table.

Two novices were setting up their first-ever game. They knew where to place the red balls and the cue (white) ball, but hadn't a clue which colored ball went on which spot. They decided to guess, and spot the balls anywhere. How many possible different ways are there of spotting the six colored balls?

7 MAGIC-WORD SQUARE

This is a sample of a 5 × 5 magic square, so called because the same five words can be read across and down.

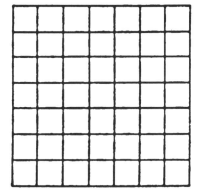

Magic-word squares become rarer as the number of letters increases. An 8 × 8 square has been compiled, but so far no 9 × 9 or 10 × 10 square has been discovered, and we doubt if these are possible in English (or in any other language).

Here are clues for a 7 × 7 magic square. All the answers are seven-letter words, and they read the same both across and down when placed correctly in the grid.

CLUES (IN NO PARTICULAR ORDER)

Devour greedily
False to his allegiance
Lamp
Settles
Stricter
One who enters profession
Eccentric

8 DIAMOND CROSSWORD

Answers run in the direction of compass points.

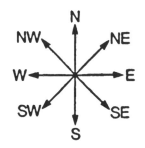

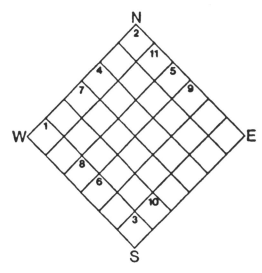

CLUES

1 E	Palatable liquid	
1 S.E.	Musical piece	
1 N.E.	Harsh	
2 S.	Errors	
2 S.E.	Rubs out	
3 N.E.	Spies	
4 E.	Age	
4 S.	Volcano	
4 S.W.	Evenings	
4 N.E.	Sooner than	

5 W.	Exist	
5 S.	Pain	
6 N.	Before	
6 E.	Consumed	
7 E.	Animal doctors	
7 S.	Vehicle	
8 E.	Midday	
9 S.	Religion	
10 N.E.	Males	
11 S.E.	Burns to the ground	

9 DOUBLE CROSS ALPHABET

Insert the 26 letters of the alphabet into each grid once only. Only one word is common to both grids.

CLUES (IN NO PARTICULAR ORDER)

Narrow strip of leather	Addict
Moral corruption	Foot covered
A mineral	Annoy
Act craftily	Leather strip
Nest in rank	Touchy
Moisture	Falsehood
Value of heaven	Shoots

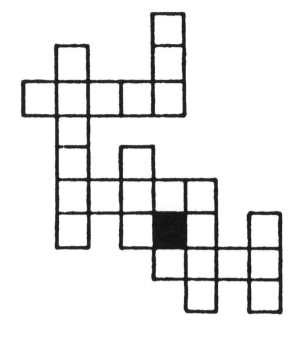

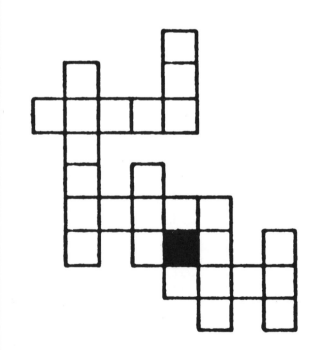

10 CRYPTOGRAM

One word keyed, 12

HDHJKJOT KUL ALOAHKJNO NS H AUNMK AUHMY
AUNWQ, SMNX H QULHY HOR QUJYYF QUN-
YYLM NO H PJT PIHQW PINQW.
D.A. TJIPLMK
(KUL XJWHRN)

11 CRYPTOGRAM

Message keyed, 5-2-10

JIXRSJK SH LH GLHC LH SX NIIUH.
GZGFCXRSJK XLUGH NIJKGF XRLJ CIY
GBEGPX. SQ LJCXRSJK PLJ KI AFIJK, SX
ASNN MI HI; LJM LNALCH LX XRG AIFHX
EIHHSONG VIVGJX.

VFERC'H NLA

12 ABOVE OR BELOW

Where would you place 9 and 10 to keep the
sequence going?

1 2   6
  3 4 5 7 8

13 DISPLACEMENT

I floated a lump of metal in a plastic bowl in a
bath of water. Then I took the lump of metal
out and dropped it into the water. Did the
water level rise, fall, or remain the same?

14 THE BARREL OF RUM PUZZLE

"This barrel of rum is more than half full," says
Charlie. "No it's not," says Harry. "It's less than
half full."

Without any measuring implements, how can
they easily determine who is correct? There is
no lid on the barrel and no rum can be taken
out.

15 MISSING NUMBERS

Fill in the missing numbers:

4	7	8	3	8	5
6	5			7	4
8	1	8	6	2	
3	6	5	8	7	6
	7	2	6	3	7
8	4	7	4	7	5

16 THE 3-2-1 HORROR

Study the numbers in each horizontal row and then decide what, logically, the missing numbers should be.

| 3 3 1 | 2 3 1 1 | 1 2 13 2 1 |

| 2 3 3 | 1 2 2 3 | 1 1 2 2 1 3 |

| 1 2 1 | 1 1 1 2 1 1 | |

17 ANAGRAMS

All of these are one-word anagrams:

(a) EASTER EGG
(b) IS A CHARM
(c) REMOTE
(d) OPEN CLAIM
(e) HOTEL SUITE
(f) BORDELLO
(g) ADMIRER
(h) INTO MY ARM
(i) THERE WE SAT
(j) RESTFUL

18 PYRAMID

You must enter each room once only, in a continuous route, and spell out a 15-letter word. You may enter the corridor as many times as you wish.

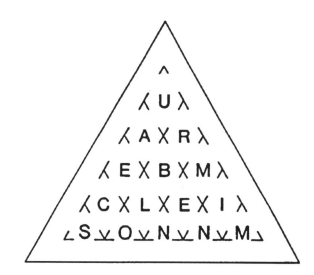

19 ANTIGRAMS

"Antigrams" are anagrams in which the letters of a word are reorganized to form a word or phrase meaning the opposite. All the answers here are one word.

(a) I LIMIT ARMS
(b) IS IT LEGAL? NO
(c) FINE TONIC
(d) NICE TO IMPORTS
(e) AIM TO CONDEMN
(f) TEAR NO VEILS
(g) ARCHSAINTS
(h) ARE ADVISERS
(i) MORE TINY
(j) CARE IS NOTED

20 THE MAGIC "37"

If the digits 1-9 are placed in the grid as follows:

4	6	2
7	1	9
8	5	3

A total of 16 different numbers will be formed if each horizontal, vertical, and corner-to-corner line is read both forward and backward.

Rearrange the digits 1-9 in the grid in such a way that if each of the 16 three-figure numbers is extended to form a palindromic six-figure number (e.g. 462264 or 264462), then each of those 16 six-figure numbers will divide exactly by 37.

21 ELEVENS

Place the digits into the grids so that each horizontal and vertical line is divisible by 11 exactly, when read either forwards or backwards. Remember, no multiplication or division is necessary. All you need to do is ensure that the alternate digits in each horizontal and vertical line, when added together, equal the same; for example, 5148, or, 5 + 4 = 1 + 8.

(a)
1, 1,
3, 3, 3, 3, 3,
4, 4, 5, 5,
6, 6, 8, 8, 9.

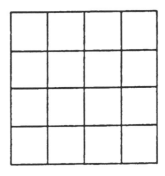

(b)
1, 1, 1,
2,
3, 3, 3, 3, 3,
4, 5, 5, 6, 7, 8, 9.

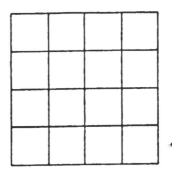

22 WORDS

In each of the following, which is the odd one out?

(a) DEBT, AIM, KNOW, TWO, SCENE, AEON

(b) SING, RECORD, TEAR, REBEL, WIND

23 FIGURES

Which of these figures is the odd one out?

(a)   **(b)**   **(c)**   **(d)**   **(e)**

24 ALPHABET

Use the 26 letters of the alphabet once each to complete these words.

ABCDEFGHIJKLMNOPQRSTUVWXYZ

1 _ A _ E
2 L _ _ _ R I _ _
3 Z _ _ E
4 _ O U _ _
54 _ O Y
65 _ Y _ E
7 _ E _ R _
8 _ _ A _ I _ _
9 E _ I _ _

25 PAIR WORDS

Here are two lists of words.

Each word in List A has two possible pair words in List B.

There are two possible solutions. Pair a word from each list until you have 9 pairs.

LIST A	LIST B
ARROW	TRACTOR
TURRET	RIVER
FARM	BULL'S-EYE
YARBOROUGH	BOW
SAND	TANK
YEW	CARDS
VEHICLE	CASTLE
RIPARIAN	BANK
JACK	WOOD
	BRIDGE

26 TEN CLUES

What do all of the answers to the following clues have in common?

1	DOCTRINE	6	GAME
2	FEELER	7	FRAME
3	HOLDING FAST	8	THIN
4	STRESS	9	MEANING
5	OFFER	10	DWELLING

27 FOLLOW THAT

The following words form a logical progression:

THAT
DOCUMENTATION
MEANDER
GRAVY
EMBANKMENT
JUBILEE

Which is next: EXTERMINATION, OCCUPATION, GRAMMAR, or ZOO?

28 U-FRAME

Each horizontal and vertical row includes the consonants of a word which can be completed by adding a number of "U" vowels. The two-figure number at the end of each line indicates the number of consonants and "U" vowels, e.g., 2-1 indicates two consonants and one "U" vowel.

	1	2	3	4	5	6	7	
1	R	S	J	T	G	R	K	2·1
2	S	S	C	F	S	C	C	4·2
3	C	C	P	M	P	B	S	5·2
4	S	G	S	L	P	F	Z	2·2
5	C	R	B	S	M	S	C	5·3
6	M	C	C	F	L	S	C	4·3
7	T	T	P	S	T	F	H	3·1
	4·1	3·2	3·1	4·1	3·1	3·1	4·1	

Each letter in the grid is used only once, and all letters must be used. (The consonants to be used in each line are not necessarily in the correct order or adjacent.)

CLUES

ACROSS
1 CONTAINER
2 NORTH AFRICAN DISH
3 BE OVERCOME
4 BANTU
5 FEMALE DEMON
6 CLOUD
7 STRIKE GOLF BALL

DOWN
1 ROOF SUPPORT
2 SPIRITUAL TEACHERS
3 HORN OF CRESCENT
4 MATERIAL
5 LIGHT SHOE
6 BIRD
7 PART OF LATHE

29 NUMBER RHYME

If my three were a four,
And my one were a three,
What I am would be nine less
Than half what I'd be.
I'm only three digits,
Just three in a row,
So what in the world must I be?
Do you know?
(I am a whole number.)

30 FIELD

This field, 112m x 75m, can be split into 13 square plots. Fill in the dimensions. All dimensions are in whole whole meters. (Not to scale)

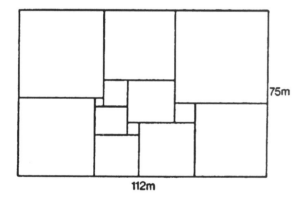

75m

112m

31 SNEAK THIEF

A sneak thief has been at work in a classroom. When the pupils return from lunch, 80 percent have lost a pencil, 85 percent have lost a pen, 74 percent have lost a ruler, and 68 percent have lost an eraser.

What percentage, at least, must have lost all four items?

32 FRACTION

Arrange the following digits, 1-2-3-4-5-6-7-8-9, to form a single fraction that equals one third.

33 "100" PUZZLE

Without changing the order of the digits, form a calculation equal to 100. Only four plus and/or minus signs can be inserted between the digits.

9 8 7 6 5 4 3 2 1 = 100

34 DECIMATE

When the Roman army needed to punish a large number of men, every tenth soldier was executed—hence, the word "decimate." You are one of a band of 1,000 mutinous pirates, captured and tied to numbered posts arranged in a circle. The first is to be executed, then each alternate pirate until one remains, who will go free. Which number post would you choose?

35 DECIMAL POINTS

In this addition sum only one decimal point is in its correct position. Alter four of the decimal points to make the sum correct.

        36.7
        1874.5
        109.6
        14.8

        383.11

36 ACROSTIC

Solve the clues, place each letter in its appropriate position in the grid, and a Shakespeare quotation will appear.

LING (7)
AVAILS ONESELF OF (4)
REMAINS (7)
HAUGHTY (6)
AMOUNTING TO (10)
MUSCLE CRAMP (7)
SEEKS JUSTICE FROM (4)
ENTRANCE (9)
A CARDINAL NUMBER (4)
GREAT HAPPINESS (8)
BE OF VALUE (5)
FAINTS (6)
LIFT UP (7)
FOAM (5)
DOES WRONG (7)
CUT WITH AXE (3)
OF THE THIGH (7)

2F	8B	2C	1E	12C	3F	18D			
13F	5F	12A	14E						
15D	15B	10F	7B	19F	17F	7A			
15C	21E	7E	15A	10B	13E				
17B	16F	2B	14F	7D	4F	20E	14B	5B	5A
14C	7C	12E	10E	13B	9D	18F			
19D	17D	6F	17A						
20B	3C	18E	9A	11D	6A	16D	7F	6E	
3C	1B	12B	19C						
1A	9C	17C	6B	1C	4B	3D	4E		
9E	8F	18E	1D	13A					
19E	16A	2A	4D	2D	8A				
10D	6D	16C	18C	14D	11C	17E			
11A	3A	11B	1F	18B					
12F	3B	20A	13C	20F	8D	20C			
2E	9F	11E							
13D	3E	8C	19A	5C	19B	14A			

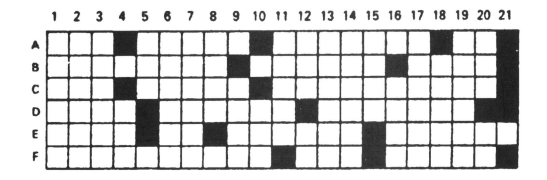

(grid columns 1–21, rows A–F)

37 I'LL MAKE A WISE PHRASE

Place each word in the correct position in the correct grid and two Shakespeare quotations will appear.

A, A, ART, BIRD, BUT, DAY, DID, EVER, FAULTS, GIVE, GODS, HAUNCH, HUMANITY, IN, LIFTING, MAKE, MEN, NEVER, OF, OF, RARER, SINGS, SOME, SPIRIT, STEER, SUMMER, THE, THE, THOU, TO, UP, US, WHICH, WILL, WINTER, YOU.

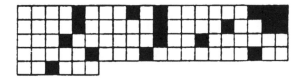

King Henry IV, Part 2, IV. iv

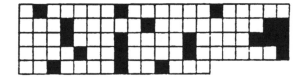

Antony and Cleopatra, V. i.

38 DOUBLE ACROSTIC

Each couplet provides the clue to a word. When you have solved them, read down the first and last letters of the five words to reveal two further words.

Very brief a note to play,
Liquid measure either way.
Here's a title I suspect,
Turkey, Sir, yes with respect.
Just an idea or a fancy,
Opinion, belief or view you can see.
Listen closely hear the clue,
You paid attention, good for you!
Now a line, or coalition,
Revolve around it with precision.

39 ALL AT SEA

Start at the center square and work from square to square horizontally, vertically, and diagonally to find eight ships. Every square is used once only. Finish at the top right-hand square.

H	T	I	E	J	C	H
E	G	E	R	T	U	T
R	Y	A	F	A	N	E
T	C	N	✳	G	K	K
H	A	K	O	I	R	R
T	E	L	O	R	F	E
R	S	P	T	A	W	L

NOW CHECK YOUR ANSWERS AND RECORD YOUR SCORE.

TEST 2

TIME LIMIT: 40 MINUTES

1 Which anagram is the odd one out?

(A) REDRESS
(B) BLEAT
(C) BROADSIDE
(D) GARDEN
(E) LOOTS

2 Which tumbler is wrong?

3 From a certain station a northbound train ran every ten minutes throughout the day; a southbound train also ran every ten minutes throughout the day. A man went to the station every day at random times and caught the first train that arrived. On average he caught the northbound train nine times out of ten. Why was this?

4 What is x?

3	4	13
8	8	56
1	5	24
9	7	40
2	2	2
6	4	10
7	5	18
4	9	77
5	3	X

5 Which is the odd word out?

(A) MICA   (D) TOMB
(B) ACRE   (E) TIED
(C) SOLD   (F) UPON

6 And which is the odd one out here?

(A) GAMMA   (D) NAFTA
(B) KAPPA   (E) OMEGA
(C) IOTA   (F) ETA

7 If ELK/GNU = ⅔ and HEN/FOX = ⅗, what is this?

PIG/RAM

8 Pair the words in the first column with the words in the second column, finishing with ten related pairs.

(A) STONE	(1) DAY
(B) FREE	(2) MOON
(C) HARVEST	(3) WALL
(D) MONUMENTAL	(4) HAND
(E) CORN	(5) FALL
(F) HALF	(6) FESTIVAL
(G) RIGHT	(7) HEARTED
(H) SECOND	(8) STONE
(I) SUN	(9) MINDED
(J) BIG	(10) FLOWER

9 What are x, y and z?

76 69 52 65 60 45 54 51 38
43 42 31 32 33 24 X Y Z

10 What are x and y?

S	20
8	J
W	25
16	T
A	4
5	K
C	7
x	L
A	y
4	N

11 Which of the figures at the bottom should come next?

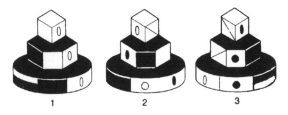

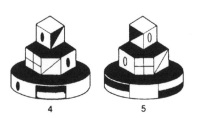

?

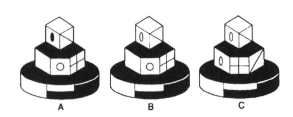

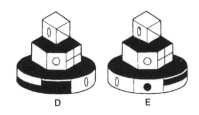

12 A rotates clockwise all the time, one position at a time. If it stops on an odd number, ball B moves one place counterclockwise; if A stops on an even number, B moves three places clockwise. If ball B stops on an even number, ball C moves three places clockwise; if B stops on an odd number, C moves five places counterclockwise.

At the end of six moves what place will be spelled out by ball C?

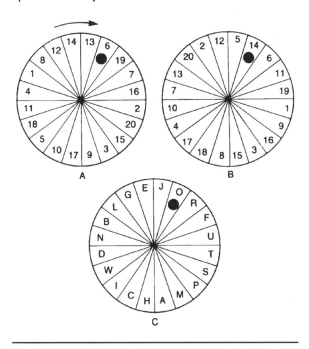

A

B

C

13 What time will this clock show in 3½ hours' time, assuming that it loses four seconds in every hour? (State the exact time.)

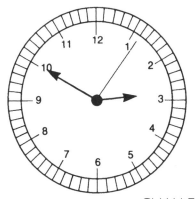

14 A turns clockwise, two positions at a time. B turns counterclockwise, three positions at a time. After six moves, what will be the total of the two front faces? (The concealed numbers progress in the same way as the visible numbers: 7, 9 and 11 on A and 8, 10, 12 on B.)

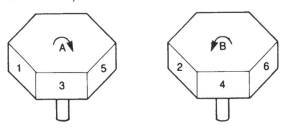

15 Assuming that the top two houses are correct, which of those below are wrong?

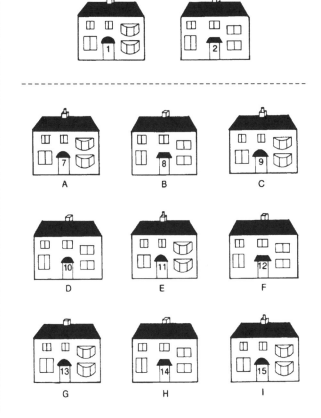

A

B

C

D

E

F

G

H

I

1 If CROCUS is 7, LUPIN is 12 and ROSE is 17, what is TULIP?

2 Which of the designs at the bottom should occupy the empty space?

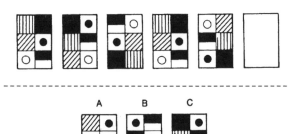

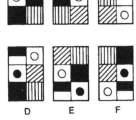

3 What comes next in this series?

625   1296   25   365   –

4 Study the top cards and find what city is represented by the bottom cards.

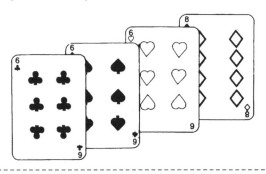

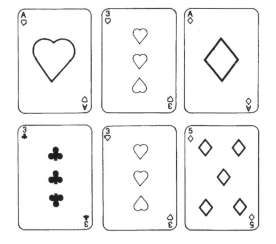

5 Find one word to fit the first definition and then, change one letter to make the word fit the second definition.

(A) Tell – Physically weak through age

(B) Settle – Laugh to scorn

(C) Month – Rightly

(D) Season ticket holder – Calculating machine

(E) Oval – Outshine

(F) Silent – Bed covering

(G) Corrupt – Holy man

(H) Emperor – It means nothing

6 What goes into the empty brackets?

144 (3625) 125
96 (1618) 126
112 ( ) 144

7 What are x, y and z?

C I F E	H F G B	G E C H
<u>B F E A</u>	<u>C I E D</u>	<u>C A B D</u>
F F A F	A B F B F	x y z 4

8 Two poets are mixed up in each of these:

(A) DRY NORTH-WEST NOW, SON.
(B) DAFT LIMEHOUSE? YES!
(C) A LEVEL C.O. SO HUMAN!

9 Which of those at the bottom comes next?

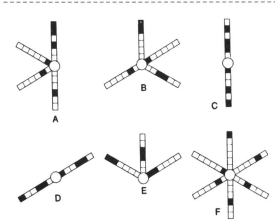

10 What is the last term in the bottom line?

1/5	.4	3/5	.8	1
1/3	1	1 2/3	2.33	3
1/4	1	1 3/4	2.5	3 1/4
1/8	.625	1 1/8	1.625	—

11 If NAZY equals WEM, FLX equals KE and HVW equals YAK, which of the sequences below equals AZVN?

(A) TEX
(B) HLF
(C) KWE
(D) NYZ
(E) FLE

12 What is x?

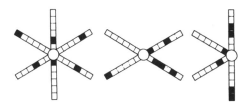

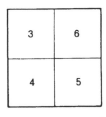

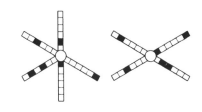

13 Write pairs of words for the definitions given below. In each pair the words are spelled differently but pronounced the same:

(A) SWAN
(B) SMALL ISLAND
(C) DINED
(D) DARK PERIOD
(E) CIRCLET
(F) EGYPTIAN RULER
(G) MAN
(H) HIDING-PLACE
(I) MAXIMUM HEIGHT
(J) VEND

(1) SEAL
(2) SMALL HOLE
(3) NUMBER
(4) CHESS PIECE
(5) SQUEEZE
(6) CARD GAME
(7) POST
(8) MONEY
(9) FIXING
(10) STALL

14 What should go into the empty brackets?

305	(6165)	13
280	(5670)	14
145	(2925)	5
70	(1415)	3
25	( )	1

15 If PEACE is 30, what letter will complete this word and give the same total?

HEA–

NOW CHECK YOUR ANSWERS AND RECORD YOUR SCORE.

TEST 4

TIME LIMIT: 30 MINUTES

1 If MEN equals 47147 and TEA equals 4471, which of the numbers below represents HIT?

(A) 471
(B) 1147
(C) 774
(D) 1441
(E) 447

2 Pair the emblems on the left with the places on the right.

(A) RED SUN   (1) CANADA
(B) LEEK   (2) GREAT BRITAIN
(C) SHAMROCK   (3) JAPAN
(D) MAPLE LEAF   (4) IRELAND
(E) STARS & STRIPES (5) WALES
(F) UNION JACK   (6) UNITED STATES

3 Copy this grid and complete this crossword puzzle from the words listed on the left.

ANGER
ASTER
BATON
BLUSH
CARRY
CHASM
CIGAR
COMIC
CRASH
CUBIC
HONEY
HURRY
MONEY
ORGAN

4 Which of the figures at the bottom should follow 3 at the top?

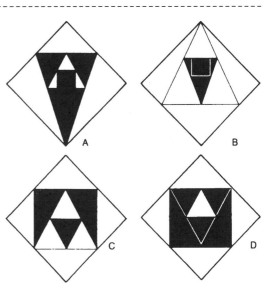

5 What are x and y?

A	A	B	B	12
A	B	C	B	19
B	x	A	B	17
y	C	A	A	18
13	22	17	14	

6 Which book is wrong?

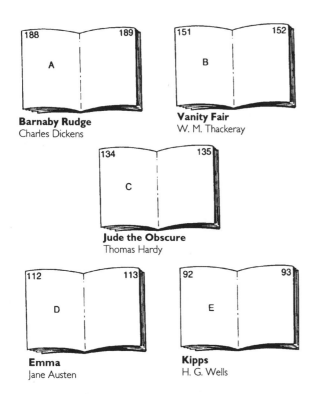

Barnaby Rudge
Charles Dickens
188 189 A

Vanity Fair
W. M. Thackeray
151 152 B

Jude the Obscure
Thomas Hardy
134 135 C

Emma
Jane Austen
112 113 D

Kipps
H. G. Wells
92 93 E

7 Which number from 1 to 9 is x?

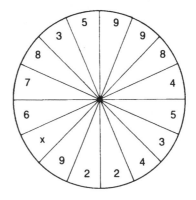

8 Which is the odd one out?

(A) I AM LAW
(B) SWAN BOAT
(C) I AM A NIB
(D) LOST HOE
(E) NEAR GIANT

9 What is x?

1	2	3	2	10	12
2	5	12	10	16	13
1	2	1	x	10	24

10 Multiply the square root of the highest number by the square of the lowest number.

144	6	169	7	152
5	166	9	158	8
3	168	4	167	10

11 A closet has been removed from a room, leaving a space on the floor with no carpet. The rest of the floor is carpeted, and fortunately there are some pieces of carpet left over. Which two pieces will fit the empty space and exactly match the existing carpet?

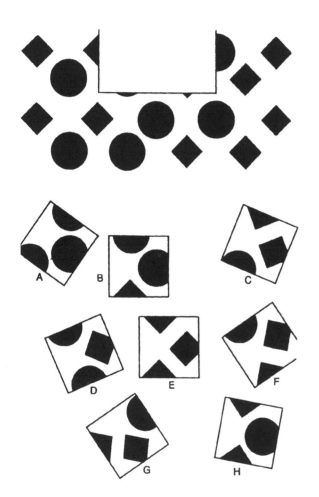

12 What is x?

4 9 1 3 2 2 3 5 5 7 9 x

13 Pair the given name in the first column with the surnames in the second column.

(A) CHARLES	(1) MILTON
(B) WILLIAM	(2) MARLOWE
(C) JAMES	(3) LEACOCK
(D) HILAIRE	(4) KINGSLEY
(E) JOHN	(5) CHAUCER
(F) CHRISTOPHER	(6) BLAKE
(G) EDWARD	(7) SPENSER
(H) EDMUND	(8) BELLOC
(I) STEPHEN	(9) BARRIE
(J) GEOFFREY	(10) LEAR

14 Which word is spelled wrong?

(A) EMBARRASS
(B) SIEGE
(C) ACCOMMODATE
(D) HARASS
(E) DECEIVE
(F) PUSILANIMOUS
(G) CATALYST

15 Here is part of a jigsaw puzzle on which a triangle is marked. Which is the missing piece?

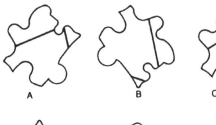

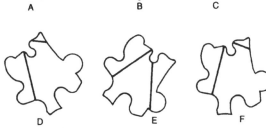

A   B   C

D   E   F

1 What number goes into the empty brackets?

916   (160)   916
971   (177)   879
245   (   )   511

2 Which is the odd one out?

(A) $^{15}/_{16}$
(B) $^{11}/_{13}$
(C) $^{2}/_{3}$
(D) $^{4}/_{7}$
(E) $^{5}/_{17}$

3 Go from DOVER to PARIS in six moves, changing one letter at a time.

  D O V E R
1 _ _ _ _ _
2 _ _ _ _ _
3 _ _ _ _ _
4 _ _ _ _ _
5 _ _ _ _ _
6 P A R I S

4 What comes between 16 and 4 in this series?

6561   256   81   16   –   4   3

5 Which is the odd one out?

(A) AFGHAN
(B) STUPOR
(C) INDIAN
(D) DEFIANT
(E) LAUGHING

6 Without using a straight edge, if AB and XY are joined, which number will be nearest to the point of intersection?

A   X
●   ●

        9
       4   1
            8
    3   5
     2   7   6

●Y   ●B

7 Complete this series:

1   2   3   5   8   13   21   34   55   –

8 Which is the odd one out?

(A) STOP   (E) KNAR
(B) YARD   (F) NIPS
(C) PANS   (G) TRAY
(D) EMIR

9 A train leaves Womensville for Manstown with twice as many women passengers as men. At Middleton 16 women get off and 17 men get on. There are now the same number of each. How many passengers left Womensville?

10 What letter takes the place of x?

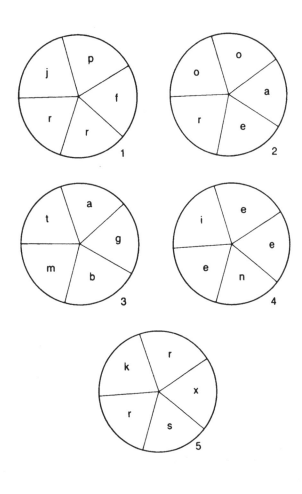

1

2

3

4

5

12

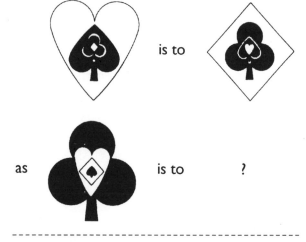

is to

as

is to   ?

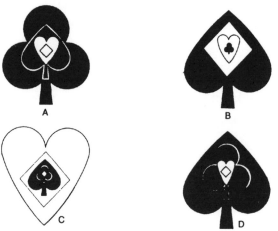

A

B

C

D

---

11 Which is the odd one out?

(A) TEAL
(B) COB
(C) PEN
(D) CYGNET
(E) SWAN

13 Six of these keys will open the door. Which one won't?

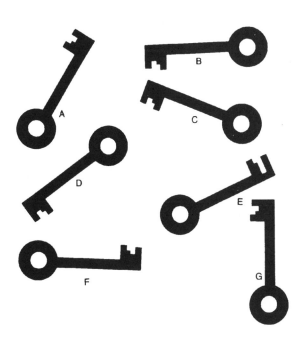

14 Pair these words to make nine titles of books by Charles Dickens:

(A) LITTLE	(1) RUDGE
(B) PICKWICK	(2) COPPERFIELD
(C) EDWIN	(3) TIMES
(D) BARNABY	(4) CHUZZLEWIT
(E) NICHOLAS	(5) PAPERS
(F) HARD	(6) HOUSE
(G) BLEAK	(7) DROOD
(H) DAVID	(8) DORRIT
(I) MARTIN	(9) NICKLEBY

15 Which screw is different?

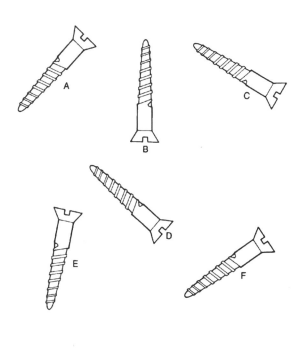

NOW CHECK YOUR ANSWERS AND RECORD YOUR SCORE.

1 Solve the clues, and two boys' names will appear in the vertical columns headed x and y.

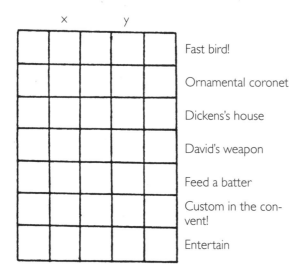

Fast bird!

Ornamental coronet

Dickens's house

David's weapon

Feed a batter

Custom in the convent!

Entertain

2 Which triangle is wrong?

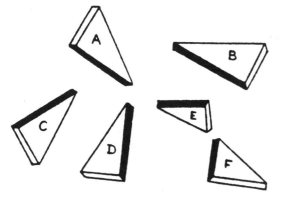

3 Square the third-lowest even number and subtract the result from the third-highest odd number:

9 67 4 11 58 66 2 65 1 8 10 41 6 71 5 12 25 3 7 41 32 70 69 68

4 Which is the odd one out?

(A) FEDERATION (B) OUTSPAN (C) CANOPY (D) COUPON (E) REDCAP

5 What should go into the empty segment?

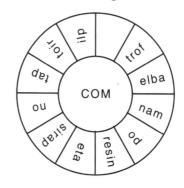

6 Whose face is in the mirror?

7 What is X?

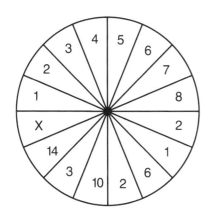

8 TWO different words can be made by inserting two different letters into the blank space. You must give both words.

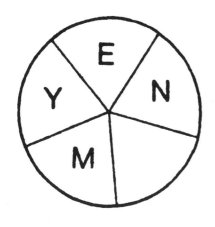

9 Which words go into the brackets? Each word must logically follow the previous word and precede the next word, e.g., putting (GREEN) land.

COMMON
(A) (   )
KICK
(B) (   )
PIPE
(C) (   )
BACK
(D) (   )
STATION
(E) (   )
PIECE
(F) (   )
TIME
(G) (   )
SPOON
(H) (   )
STOCK
(I) (   )
WISE
(J) (   )
DOWN

10 Which of the numbered circles at the bottom should be placed at A, B, C, and D?

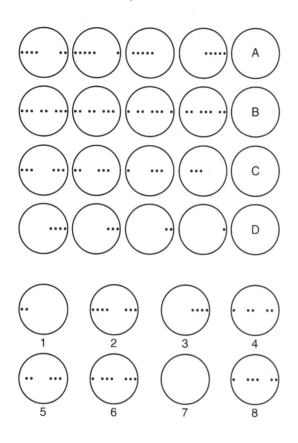

11 What is the difference between the lowest number and the average of all the numbers?

3 9 12 15 18 25 30

12 Here are seven common words. Which is the odd one out?

(A) DIM
(B) MIND
(C) MILL
(D) LIVID
(E) VIM
(F) MIX
(G) CIVIL

13 Give words to fit the definitions. Each word removes one letter from the word above it.

_ _ _ _ _ _ _	Place for cigarettes
_ _ _ _ _ _	Not on the right course
_ _ _ _ _	Go off course
_ _ _ _	Shallow Vessel
_ _ _	Sea-fish
_ _	Affirmative
_	Musical note

14 Which three pieces below will make the face above?

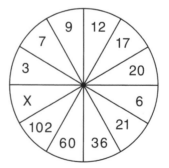

15 What is X?

NOW CHECK YOUR ANSWERS AND RECORD YOUR SCORE.

I Which cup is the odd one out?

2 What is the TOTAL number of spots on the rear side?

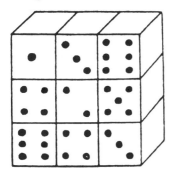

3 The same four letters in a different order will complete these words:

(A) - - - - ted
(B) l - - - -
(C) - - - - t
(D) ey - - - - l
(E) culp - - - -

4 What comes next?

124 81 6 32 641 2 -

5 Which is the odd one out?

(A) HEARD   (D) URCHIN
(B) RUSHING   (E) DIAGNOSED
(C) CLIPPER   (F) MONEYED

6 What are a, b, c, and d?

3   27   1   32   4   26   3   29
5   25   5   26   6   a   b   c   d

7 What letter should go into the empty space?

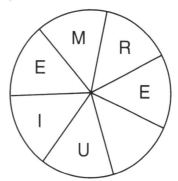

8 What letters should be substituted for X and Y on the last cube?

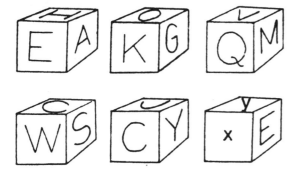

9 If this shape were folded along the dotted lines, it could be made into a cube:

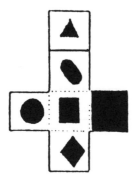

like this:

If this cube were turned upside-down, which of these faces would appear at the top?

A   B   C

10 What are x, y, and z?

A 1 3 L 12 6 M 13 9 O 15 12 S 19 x y z

11 The same word can precede each of these word-endings:

(A) CASS (B) BON (C) TON (D) GO (E) EEN

12 Examine the first three car license plates and then complete the last one:

GFH 759

FGH

13 What are x, y, and z?

3	42	40
7	52	53
12	63	68
18	75	85
25	88	104
X	102	125
42	Y	148
52	133	Z

14 If this design were turned ninety degrees counter-clockwise and held in front of a mirror, which of the designs below would be reflected?

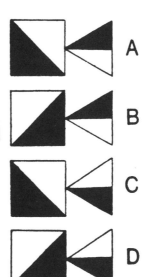

A

B

C

D

15 All of these might be found in a subway station, but you must unscramble them first:

(A) KENERKLOCTO (B) PRAMLOFT (C) LETISRUNT (D) TORDUCNOC (E) EXPRESS

NOW CHECK YOUR ANSWERS AND RECORD YOUR SCORE.

1 Which is the odd one out

(A) IAMBUS

(B) TROCHEE

(C) RONDURE

(D) PAEON

(E) SPONDEE

(F) DACTYL

2 Which one is different?

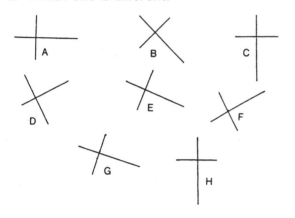

3 What comes next in the series?

16 72 38 94 50 -

4 The black ball moves one position at a time clockwise. The white ball moves two positions at a time counter-clockwise. a) In how many moves will they be together again? b) In which corner will they be when they meet?

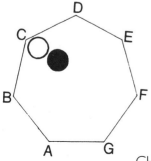

5 What is X?

1 2 3 4 5 6 7 8 7 14 1 2 2 1 8 7 10 3 4 18 2 1 8 6 10 3
4 18 2 1 8 6 8 5 11 12 2 21 3 4 2 11 6 3 13 1 2 10 2 5
5 1 6 10 2 X

6 A sentence may conceal a "hidden" word. Thus, in this sentence the word ENSIGN is "hidden": HeathENS IGNore Christians. What "voices" are hidden in these sentences?

7 If the two dotted lines are placed together, what will be the result?

8 What are x and y?

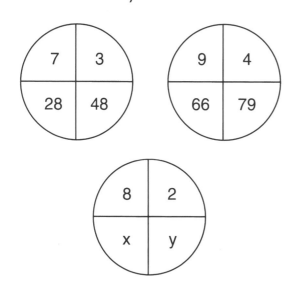

9 Arrange these in order of length, starting with the shortest:

(A) DECAMETER (B) CENTIMETER (C) MILLIMETER (D) KILOMETER (E) DECIMETER (F) METER (G) HECTOMETER

10 Which flag is wrong and WHY?

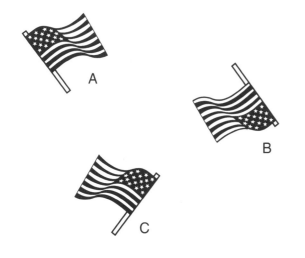

11 Who is the odd man out?

(A) MARCONI (B) CARUSO (C) EDISON (D) BAIRD (E) WHITNEY

12 What are x and y?

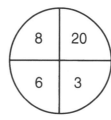 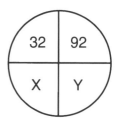

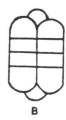 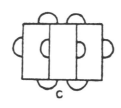

13 Which is the odd one out?

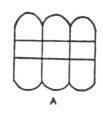 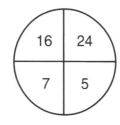

 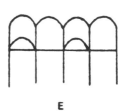

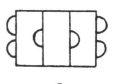

14 What comes next in this series?

1072 1055 1021 953 817 545 -

15 Complete the final square:

935	824	713
148	365	582

KWG	JVF	IUE
UAM	WCJ	YEG

X7Z	W6Y	
3U7	5W4	

NOW CHECK YOUR ANSWERS AND RECORD YOUR SCORE.

1 What is X?

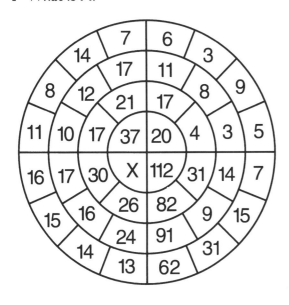

2 Which one is wrong?

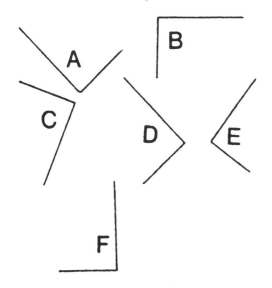

3 Which of the figures at the bottom should follow the six figures at the top?

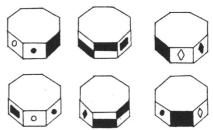

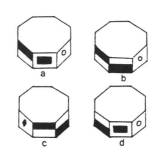

4 What comes next in this series?

I III VI X XV XXI XXVIII

5 Complete this crossword puzzle, choosing the words from the list below

TULIP
BURST
QUEST
EAGLE
RATIO
FULLY
LEVER
ANGER
QUART
TORCH
TEETH

6 Which is the odd one out?

(A) ESOPHAGUS   (D) STERNUM
(B) SCAPULA   (E) ULNA
(C) CLAVICLE   (F) HUMERUS

7 17 is to 101 as 13 is to 77, and as 19 is to __?

8 Join these words to form 10 other words or word pairs:

TEN	DEN	ORC	MATE	LIGHT
SCHOOL	SUN	HOME	HID	DON
WAY	DAY	HIGH	KEY	BOY
BULB	MON	LAND	HARD	CHECK

9 Which currency belongs to which country?

(A) KRONE   (1) SPAIN
(B) LIRA   (2) DENMARK
(C) PESETA   (3) PORTUGAL
(D) ESCUDO   (4) RUSSIA
(E) RUBLE   (5) ITALY

10

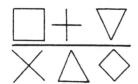

is to

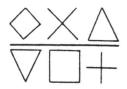

as $\dfrac{351}{762}$ is to?

11 What comes next in this series?

1 0 11 E 8 E 12T 2T 3T 4 -

12 All of these shapes—except one—are of the same area. Which is the exception, and is it of greater or lesser area?

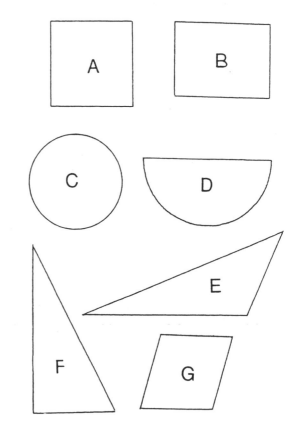

13 Which of these is wrong?

A
> "A thing of beauty
> is a joy for ever."
>
> John Keats, 1795-1821

B
> "If you can keep your head
> when all about you/Are
> losing theirs…"
>
> Rudyard Kipling, 1865-1936

C
> "My heart's in the
> the Highlands, my
> heart is not here."
>
> Robert Burns, 1739-1796

D
> "If music be the food
> of love, play on."
>
> William Shakespeare, 1564-1616

14 What does the third clock show?

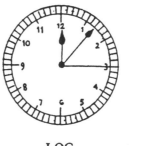
LOG

HUT

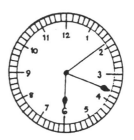

15 Which number is nearest to the number which is midway between the lowest and the highest number?

11	84	41	9	79
81	7	36	51	47
88	12	8	89	10

NOW CHECK YOUR ANSWERS AND RECORD YOUR SCORE.

TEST 1 ANSWERS

1 b. The outer dot moves clockwise, first by one position, then two positions, then three, etc. The inner dot moves counter-clockwise, first by one position, then two positions, then three, etc.

2 d. To complete every possible grouping in three of the four different symbols.

3 Looking across, the curved lines merge and the straight lines disappear. Looking down, the reverse happens. The missing square is, therefore, (f).

4 You win $59. You will always win the same number of units that heads comes down in the sequence, providing the final toss is heads.

5 There are six possible pairings of the four balls: red/red, red(1)/yellow, red(2)/yellow, red(1)/blue, red(2)/blue and yellow/blue. We know that the yellow/blue combination has not been drawn out. This leaves five possible combinations remaining, therefore the chances that the red/red pairing has been drawn out are 1 in 5.

6 720, i.e. 6! or $6 \times 5 \times 4 \times 3 \times 2 \times 1$.

7
Nestles	Lantern
Entrant	Engorge
Strange	Sterner
Traitor	

8 1.E. Sauces, 1.S.E. Sonata, 1.N.E. Severe, 2.S. Errata, 2.S.E. Erases, 3.N.E. Agents, 4.E. Era, 4.S. Etna, 4.S.W. Eves, 4.N.E. Ere, 5.W. Are, 5.S. Ache, 6.N. Ante, 6.E. Ate, 7.E. Vets, 7.S. Van, 8.E. Noon, 9.S. Zen, 10.N.E. Gents, 11.S.E. Razes.

9 Grid One: Across – Jumpy, Thong, Vice. Down – Quartz, Sky, Fox, Glib, Dew. Grid Two: Across – Junky, Twigs, Come. Down – Quartz, Ply, Fib, Shod, Vex.

10 Awaiting the sensation of a short sharp shock. From a cheap and chippy chopper on a big black block.

W.S. Gilbert

(The Mikado)

Word keyed (ALITERON) Alliteration.

11 Nothing is as easy as it looks. Everything takes longer than you expect. If anything can go wrong, it will do so; and always at the worst possible moment.

Murphy's Law

Message keyed: (PRESONGADL) — Press on regardless

12 9 below, 10 above. Numbers appearing above the line are spelled with three letters only.

13 When the metal was taken out of the bowl, the bowl displaced less water, so the water level fell by an amount corresponding to the volume of water which would have the same weight as the metal. When the metal was immersed in the water, it displaced its own volume of water and the water level rose. The amount it rose corresponded to the volume of the metal, very much less than the volume of an equal weight of water. Thus, the net result was a fall in water level.

14 They should tip the barrel onto its edge until the rum reaches the rim. If they can then see part of the bottom of the barrel, the barrel is not half full. If they cannot see part of the barrel, it is more than half full.

15 The grid should contain 1x1, 2x2, 3x3, 4x4, 5x5, 6x6, 7x7, and 8x8. The missing numbers are, therefore, 5, 6, 8, 8, and all numbers are placed in the grid so that the same number is never horizontally or vertically adjacent.

16 121 – 111211 – 311221. Each number describes the previous number, i.e., 121 then 1-1, 1-2, 1-1, then 3-1s, 1-2, 2-1s.

17 **(a)** Segregate, **(b)** Charisma, **(c)** Meteor, **(d)** Policeman, **(e)** Silhouette, **(f)** Doorbell, **(g)** Married, **(h)** Matrimony, **(i)** Sweetheart, **(j)** Fluster.

18 Incommensurable.

19 **(a)** Militarism, **(b)** Legalisation, **(c)** Infection, **(d)** Protectionism, **(e)** Commendation, **(f)** Revelations, **(g)** Anarchists, **(h)** Adversaries, **(i)** Enormity, **(j)** Desecration.

20
123   789
456 or 456   or rotations of same
789   123

21 (a) 5313
6138
4389
3564

(b) 9218
7436
3531
5313

22 (a) Aim. All the others contain silent letters.

(b) Sing. All the other words have two pronunciations.

23 (c) All the others are symmetric about a horizontal axis, i.e., they appear the same turned upside down.

24 1. Wave, 2. Limerick, 3. Zone, 4. Dough, 5. Joy, 6 Pyre, 7. Zebra, 8. Qualify, 9. Exist.

25

SOLUTION 1		SOLUTION 2	
Vehicle	Tank	Vehicle	Tractor
Turret	Castle	Turret	Tank
Sand	Bank	Sand	Castle
Riparian	River	Riparian	Bank
Yarborough	Cards	Yarborough	Bridge
Jack	Wood	Jack	Cards
Yew	Bow	Yew	Wood
Arrow	Bull's-eye	Arrow	Bow
Farm	Tractor	Farm	Bull's-eye

26 They all begin with "TEN": Tenet, Tentacle, Tenacious, Tension, Tender, Tennis, Tenter, Tenuous, Tenor, Tent.

27 Grammar. Each word starts with the letter whose position in the alphabet coincides with the number of letters in the preceding word, i.e. "THAT" has four letters; therefore, the next word starts with the fourth letter in the alphabet - D.

28 Across: 1. Jug, 2. Cuscus, 3. Succumb, 4. Zulu, 5. Succubus, 6. Cumulus, 7. Putt.

Down: 1. Truss, 2. Gurus, 3. Cusp, 4. Stuff, 5. Pump, 6. Ruff, 7. Chuck.

29 Half of "What I'd be" must be a whole number. "What I'd be" must be an even number. "What I am" cannot end in 1. There are four possible arrangements of the three digits.

	(a)	**(b)**	**(c)**	**(d)**
"What I am"	1?3	13?	31?	?13
"What I'd be"	3?4	34?	43?	?34

"What I am" is "Nine less than half what I'd be."

So ("What I am" + 9) × 2 = "What I'd be."

Examination shows that only "A" fits the bill, and "What I am" must be 183.

30

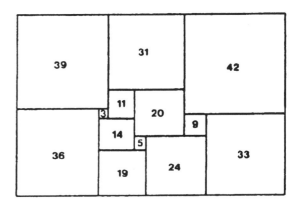

31 Add the percentages together, which gives 80 + 85 + 74 + 68 = 307 among 100 pupils. This gives 3 losses each and 4 losses to 7 pupils. The least percentage is, therefore, 7.

32 5832
‾‾‾‾‾
17496

33 98 - 76 + 54 + 3 + 21 = 100.

34 976. Take 2 to the power which gives the lowest number above 1000, which is 2^{10} = 1024.

Formula = 1024 - {(1024-1000) × 2} = 976.

35   3.67
18.745
1.096
14.8
‾‾‾‾‾
38.311

36 For these fellows of infinite tongue, that can rhyme themselves into ladies' favours, they do always reason themselves out again.

King Henry V, vii. 162

37 Thou art a summer bird which ever in the haunch of winter sings. The lifting up of day.

A rarer spirit never did steer humanity; but you, Gods, will give us some faults to make us men.

38 M ini M
E ffend I
N otio N
S oun D
A xi S

39 Freighter, Yacht, Tanker, Sloop, Trawler, Frigate, Junk, Ketch.

1 (D) **(SCORE 1 POINT).**
All except (D) are anagrams of furniture:
(A) REDRESS – DRESSER
(B) BLEAT – TABLE
(C) BROADSIDE – SIDEBOARD
(D) LOOTS – STOOL

2 F **(SCORE 1 POINT).**
The design around the top should consist entirely of diamond shapes, as in B and L. One of the diamonds has become a square.

3 The southbound train ran one minute after the northbound train **(SCORE 1 POINT).**

4 x is 4 **(SCORE 1 POINT).**
Square the middle number in each horizontal row and subtract the left-hand number to give the right-hand number. So, in the bottom row:

3 squared is	9
Subtract	5
x is	4

5 (B) **(SCORE 1 POINT).**
All others are made up with letters in reverse alphabetical order:
(A) MICA – ACIM
(C) SOLD – DLOS
(D) TOMB – BMOT
(E) TIED – DEIT
(F) UPON – NOPU

6 (D) **(SCORE 1 POINT).**
NAFTA is the acronym for the North American Free Trade Agreement. The others are letters in the Greek alphabet.
(A) GAMMA – the third letter in the Greek alphabet
(B) KAPPA – the Greek letter κ
(C) IOTA – the Greek letter ι
(E) OMEGA – the last letter (Ω) in the Greek alphabet (hence 'alpha to omega')
(F) ETA – the Greek letter η

7 1 **(SCORE 1 POINT).**
Give each letter a value according to its position in the alphabet:

$$\frac{ELK}{GNU} = \frac{5 \quad 12 \quad 11}{7 \quad 14 \quad 21}$$

$$\frac{HEN}{FOX} = \frac{8 \quad 5 \quad 14}{6 \quad 15 \quad 24}$$

$$\frac{PIG}{RAM} = \frac{16 \quad 9 \quad 7}{18 \quad 1 \quad 13}$$

Add the numbers:

28	27	32
42	45	32

Which gives us:

4 or 2	3	1
6 or 3	5	1 (which gives the answer 1)

8 (A) (3); (B) (5); (C) (6); (D) (8); (E) (10); (F) (2); (G) (9); (H) (4); (I) (1); (J) (7) **(SCORE 1 POINT IF ALL ARE CORRECT; ½ IF 8 OR 9).**

9 x is 21; y is 24; z is 17 **(SCORE 1 POINT IF ALL ARE CORRECT).**
There are three separate series. Start with the first term and take every third term thereafter:

76   65   54   43   32

As they reduce by 11 each time, the next term (x) must be 21. From the second term, proceed in the same way:

69   60   51   42   33

These reduce by 9 each time, so the next term (y) is 24. From the third term, proceed in the same way:

52   45   38   31   24

As they reduce by 7 each time the next term (z) is 17.

10 x is 4; y is 6 **(SCORE 1 POINT IF BOTH ARE CORRECT).**

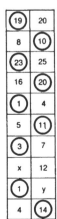

Expressing each letter as a number according to position in the alphabet, the table appears as below, with what were originally letters circled:

11 B **(SCORE 1 POINT)**.
The cube rotates clockwise; the hexagon rotates counterclockwise; the circle rotates clockwise.

12 BERLIN **(SCORE 1 POINT)**.
The moves are as follows:

	BALL A	BALL B	BALL C
1st move	19	5	B
2nd move	7	12	E
3rd move	16	6	R
4th move	2	1	L
5th move	20	3	I
6th move	15	16	N

13 6 hours, 19 minutes, 52 seconds **(SCORE 1 POINT)**.
The present time shown is 2 hours, 50 minutes, 6 seconds. Ignoring the seconds, the time in 3½ hours will be 6:20. In the meantime, the second hand will have lost 14 seconds. Instead of showing six seconds after the hour it will show eight seconds BEFORE the hour—that is, 52 seconds. This means that the minute hand will not have reached the 20-minute mark, but will have passed the 19-minute mark.

14 7 **(SCORE 1 POINT)**.
The moves result as follows:

	A	B	
1st move	7	10	
2nd move	11	4	
3rd move	3	10	
4th move	7	4	
5th move	11	10	
6th move	3	4	(Total: 7)

15 D and G **(SCORE 1 POINT IF BOTH ARE CORRECT; ½ IF ONE)**.
D (a house with an even number) should have a flat porch. G (a house with an odd number) should have a chimney stack.

NOTES

This test called for quick and clear thinking, and it is extremely unlikely that you completed all the questions within the time limit—deliberately chosen to encourage quick thinking. Because of this, and the difficult nature of the problems, inevitably low averages were recorded by the test group volunteers.

To obtain maximum points it is best to go fairly quickly through all the questions and at first answer only those which seem quite easy or quick to solve. Then you can return to those that were more difficult or would obviously have taken much longer, especially if a considerable amount of writing was necessary.

In this test 3, 7, 8, 12, 13 and 14 would have taken longest either to solve or to write down. It would have been a good idea to have left them while you worked on the others first. To have dwelt too long on any of the extra difficult ones could have deprived you of valuable time, leaving you with less time to spend on the easier problems. Remember, those six problems could have gained only six points (and that is assuming you solved them all correctly). In spending this time on them you may have sacrificed anything up to 9 points on problems which you could have solved, given time to do so.

In comparison with the tests in Group 1, you must have found this one much more difficult, though it is hoped that the experience you gain working on these tests will gradually give you a greater understanding of them.

1 18 **(SCORE 1 POINT)**.
Give each letter a value according to its position in the alphabet. Add the total of the consonants in each word and subtract the total of the value of the vowels:

T	20	U	21
L	12	I	9
P	16		30
	48		

30 subtracted from 48 gives the answer: 18.

2 D **(SCORE 1 POINT)**.
The black square moves counterclockwise, first one position, then two, then three, and so on. All other squares move in the same way.

3 6 **(SCORE 1 POINT)**.
There are two separate series here. Starting with the first term and taking alternate terms thereafter:

625   25   5

Each term is the square root of the previous term Starting with the second term:

1296   36   6

Again, each term is the square root of the previous number.

4 MOSCOW **(SCORE 1 POINT)**.
This problem is based on the fact that 26 cards make half of a full deck of playing cards, and there are also 26 letters in the alphabet. These 26 letters are represented by the cards at the top:

Clubs	Ace to 6	A to F
Spades	Ace to 6	G to L
Hearts	Ace to 6	M to R
Diamonds	Ace to 8	S to Z

Thus the cards at bottom are:

Ace of hearts	13th letter	M
3 of hearts	15th letter	O
Ace of diamonds	19th letter	S
3 of clubs	3rd letter	C
3 of hearts	15th letter	O
5 of diamonds	23rd letter	W

5 **(SCORE 1 POINT IF ALL ARE CORRECT; ½ IF 7.)**
(A) INFORM – INFIRM
(B) DECIDE – DERIDE
(C) JULY – DULY
(D) COMMUTER – COMPUTER
(E) ELLIPSE – ECLIPSE
(F) QUIET – QUILT
(G) TAINT – SAINT
(H) NERO – ZERO

6 1416 **(SCORE 1 POINT)**.
In the first line divide the number on the left by 4 and the number on the right by 5, placing the results inside the brackets. In the second line divide the number on the left by 6 and the number on the right by 7, placing the results inside the brackets. Following this procedure, in the third line divide the number on the left by 8 (14) and the number on the right by 9 (16), placing the results inside the brackets (1416).

7 x is 4; y is 4; z is 1 **(SCORE 1 POINT IF ALL ARE CORRECT)**.
Substitute numbers for letters according to the positions of the letters in the alphabet:

C I F E	3 9 6 5
B F E A	2 6 5 1
F F A F	6 6 1 6 (added)
H F G B	8 6 7 2
C I E D	3 9 5 4
A B F B F	1 2 6 2 6 (added)

It is obvious that the last one must be a subtraction because if H (8) were added to D (4) the result would be 2 in the units, whereas 4 is already given:

G E C H	7 5 3 8
C A B D	3 1 2 4
	4 4 1 4 (subtracted)

8 **(SCORE 1 POINT IF ALL ARE CORRECT; ½ IF 2.)**
(A) TENNYSON and WORDSWORTH
(B) MASEFIELD and SOUTHEY
(C) HOUSMAN and LOVELACE

9 A **(SCORE I POINT).**

From an examination of the black stripes on the vanes, the following facts emerge:

▮□□□□□○	rotates counterclockwise one position at a time
□▮□□□□○	rotates clockwise one position at a time
□□▮□□□○	rotates counterclockwise one position at a time
□□□▮□□○	rotates counterclockwise two positions at a time
□□□□▮□○	rotates clockwise two positions at a time
□□□□□▮○	rotates counterclockwise two positions at a time

10 2⅛ **(SCORE I POINT; ½ IF YOU HAVE PUT 2.125).**

Convert all the fractions into improper fractions:

1/5	2/5	3/5	4/5	5/5
1/3	3/3	5/3	7/3	9/3
1/4	4/4	7/4	10/4	13/4
1/8	5/8	9/8	13/8	(17/8)

The final fraction could be: 17/8 or 2⅛

But as in the examples, improper fractions alternate with decimal fractions throughout. Also, as in the examples, the answer must be expressed in a unit and a fraction: 2⅛

(You may have converted all the fractions into decimal fractions. In all but the second row this would have been valid, giving the final answer of 2.125. There are, however, two fallacies:

a) there are no perfect decimal fractions for ⅓ or 1⅔, as they are recurring decimals, as in 2.33 recurring;

b) the already established alternating sequence of improper and decimal fractions should be maintained.)

11 (C) **(SCORE I POINT).**

In the equations given, the number of straight strokes that form the letters is equal on each side. AZVN contains 11 straight strokes and KWE is the only one of the possible answers which also contains 11 straight strokes.

12 9 **(SCORE I POINT).**

The numbers move from one position clockwise at a time. Starting with 3 in the first square, the progression is:

3 4 5 6

Starting with 6 in the first square:

6 7 8 (9)

Starting with 5 in the first square:

5 6 7 8

Starting with 4 in the first square:

4 5 6 7

13 **(SCORE I POINT IF ALL ARE CORRECT; ½ IF 8 OR 9.)**

(A) CYGNET	(1) SIGNET
(B) ISLET	(2) EYELET
(C) ATE	(3) EIGHT
(D) NIGHT	(4) KNIGHT
(E) RING	(5) WRING
(F) PHARAOH	(6) FARO
(G) MALE	(7) MAIL
(H) CACHE	(8) CASH
(I) CEILING	(9) SEALING
(J) SELL	(10) CELL

14 55 **(SCORE I POINT).**

Divide the number on the left by 5 and multiply the number on the right by 5, entering the two results inside the brackets:

25 (55) 1

15 P **(SCORE I POINT).**

Give each letter a number according to its position in the alphabet. PEACE totals 30; HEA totals 14. Therefore, the 16th letter in the alphabet, which is P, must be added to bring the total up to 30.

NOTES

4, 8 and 9 caused the most difficulty with the majority. The coincidence that there are 26 letters in the alphabet and 26 cards in half of a pack of cards is one that you may find used elsewhere in these tests, so it is worth bearing in mind. Substitution of numbers for letters according to the position of the letters in the alphabet may also be featured again and is worth remembering for the future.

1 (A) **(SCORE 1 POINT)**.

(This problem was deliberately positioned near question 11 in the previous test to see whether you have benefited from reading the explanations.)

The number of straight lines that make up the words agrees with the number of straight lines that make up the numbers. 471 is the only figure that has the same number of strokes, six, as HIT.

2 (A) (3); (B) (5); (C) (4); (D) (1); (E) (6); (F) (2)

(SCORE 1 POINT IF ALL ARE CORRECT).

3 **(SCORE 1 POINT FOR EITHER OF THE FOLLOWING.)**

C	U	B	I	C
H		A		A
A	S	T	E	R
S		O		R
M	O	N	E	Y

C	H	A	S	M
U		S		O
B	A	T	O	N
I		E		E
C	A	R	R	Y

4 A **(SCORE 1 POINT)**.

The smallest figure in the center becomes the largest figure on the outside, while the other figures remain in the same order.

5 x is 7; y is 5 **(SCORE 1 POINT IF BOTH ARE CORRECT)**.
Incidentally, A is 2, B is 4 and C is 9.39

6 B **(SCORE 1 POINT)**.
Even page numbers always appear on the verso (left) and odd numbers always appear on the recto (right).

7 2 **(SCORE 1 POINT)**.
Starting at 7 and working clockwise, two adjacent numbers in the top semicircle are added. In the opposite segments are factors of that total:

7 + 8 = 15;	3 × 5 = 15
3 + 5 = 8;	2 × 4 = 8
9 + 9 = 18;	9 × 2 = 18

Hence:

8 + 4 = 12;	6 × 2 = 12

8 (E) **(SCORE 1 POINT)**.
This is an anagram of ARGENTINA, which is in South America. All the others are in Africa:

(A) MALAWI
(B) BOTSWANA
(C) NAMIBIA
(D) LESOTHO

9 13 **(SCORE 1 POINT)**.
The totals of the columns are:

4 9 16 ? 36 49

In other words, 2 squared, 3 squared, 4 squared, etc.

10 117 **(SCORE 1 POINT)**.

11 B and D **(SCORE 1 POINT IF BOTH ARE CORRECT; ½ IF ONE)**.

12 2 **(SCORE 1 POINT)**.
Spaced correctly the series becomes:

4 9 13 22 35 57 9(2)

After the first two numbers, each subsequent number is the total of the previous two. The sum of 35 and 57 is 92.

13 (A) (4); (B) (6); (C) (9); (D) (8); (E) (1); (F) (2); (G) (10); (H) (7); (I) (3); (J) (5) **(SCORE 1 POINT IF ALL ARE CORRECT; ½ IF 8 OR 9)**.

14 (F) **(SCORE 1 POINT)**.
It should be spelled PUSILLANIMOUS (meaning cowardly).

15 B **(SCORE 1 POINT)**.

NOTES

3, 5, 7, and 11 gave the greatest difficulty, and 3 should have taken the most time. 6 was easy unless you were preoccupied with the authors and titles, searching for a discrepancy in one or the other. 11 was tricky and definitely trying on the eyes! The patterns were so similar and it was not easy to differentiate between the left and the right halves of the bare space.

1 114 **(SCORE 1 POINT).**
The two numbers on the left inside the brackets are the sum of the digits on the left of the brackets. The number on the right inside the brackets is the difference between the sums of the digits on either side of the brackets.

2 A **(SCORE 1 POINT).**
It is the only fraction which contains an odd number (15) which is NOT a prime number. All the other fractions contain even numbers or odd numbers which are primary numbers.

3 **(SCORE 1 POINT. IF YOU HAVE USED OTHER WORDS YOU MAY SCORE 1 POINT, PROVIDED THEY ARE GENUINE.)**
  D O V E R
1 D O V E S
2 R O V E S
3 R A V E S
4 P A V E S
5 P A R E S
6 P A R I S

4 9 **(SCORE 1 POINT)**
There are two separate series here. Starting with the first term and taking alternate terms thereafter:

6561 81 9 3

Each number is the square root of the previous number.
Starting with the second term:

256 16 4

Again, each number is the square root of the previous number.

5 (C) **(SCORE 1 POINT).**
All the other words contain three consecutive letters of the alphabet.
(A) a **F G H** a n
(B) **S T U** p o r
(D) **D E F** i a n t
(E) l a u **G H I** n g

6 5 **(SCORE 1 POINT).**
This is at the EXACT point of intersection.

7 89 **(SCORE 1 POINT).**
Starting with 3, each number is the sum of the two previous numbers. Thus the final term is the sum of 34 and 55.

8 (G) **(SCORE 1 POINT).**
All the other words make words when reversed:
(A) STOP – POTS
(B) YARD – DRAY
(C) PANS – SNAP
(D) EMIR – RIME
(E) KNAR – RANK
(F) NIPS – SPIN

9 99 **(SCORE 1 POINT).**
Let x represent the number of men who get on at Womensville. The number of passengers who start the journey is $3x$.
At Middleton:
$2x-16=x+7$,
therefore:
$x=33$
We already know that twice as many women started the journey, so there must have been 66 women and 33 men.

10 n **(SCORE 1 POINT).**
Starting with j in the first circle and considering every second segment thereafter in the succeeding circles, you get: **james**
Starting with p in the first circle and proceeding in the same way: **peter**
Starting with f in the first circle and proceeding in the same way: **frank**
Starting with the first r in the first circle and proceeding in the same way: **roger**
Starting with the second r in the first circle and proceeding in the same way: **robi(n)**

11 (A) **(SCORE 1 POINT).**
A teal is a duck. All the others are swans.

12 B **(SCORE 1 POINT).**
The very small center suit becomes the large outer suit. The next smallest inner suit becomes the next largest outer suit. The next smallest inner suit becomes the next largest outer suit. The largest outer suit becomes the smallest center suit.

13 E **(SCORE 1 POINT).**
The teeth (the projections at the end) which turn the lock are different from those in the other keys.

14 (A) (8); (B) (5); (C) (7); (D) (1); (E) (9); (F) (3); (G) (6); (H) (2); (I) (4) **(SCORE 1 POINT IF ALL ARE CORRECT; ½ IF 7 OR 8).**

15 C **(SCORE 1 POINT).**
The thread turns the opposite way from the others.

NOTES

1, 4, 9 and 10 presented the most problems. If you solved 9 by algebra, as given in the explanation, it would have not have held you up for long. If you relied on trial and error it would probably have taken longer. In 10, which stumped many, the letters were deliberately printed in lower case so as to throw you off the track that they were proper names.

1 X is WILLIAM; Y is FRANCIS
(SCORE 1 POINT IF BOTH ARE CORRECT)

```
s  W  i  F  t
t  l  a  R  a
b  L  e  A  k
s  L  i  N  g
p  I  t  C  h
h  A  b  I  t
a  M  u  S  e
```

2 F **(SCORE 1 POINT)**
The shorter side is shaded. In all other triangles the longer side is shaded.

3 31 **(SCORE 1 POINT)**

4 (C) **(SCORE 1 POINT)**
CANOPY contains three consecutive letters in their correct order. Al the other words contain three consecutive letters in reverse order.

5 TNA **(SCORE 1 POINT)**
Each word starts with COM. The syllables that follow are read backwards in the outer sections: COM-FORT-ABLE COM-MAN-DO COM-MISER-ATE COM-PARIS-ON COM-PAT-RIOT COM-PLI-ANT

6 A **(SCORE 1 POINT)**

7 4 **(SCORE 1 POINT)**.
Moving clockwise and starting with number 1 in the upper half, compare each number with that in its opposite segment. 1 is doubled, giving 2 in the opposite segment; the next number (2) is halved, giving 1 in the opposite segment. The same procedure continues: double the next, then halve the next.

8 in the upper half is halved to give 4 in the opposite segment.

(An alternative solution is to double all the odd numbers and halve all the even numbers).

8 E (ENEMY) an O (MONEY) **(SCORE 1 POINT IF BOTH ARE CORRECT)**.

9 **(SCORE 1 POINT IF ALL ARE CORRECT; ½ POINT IF 3 ARE CORRECT)**.
(A) PLACE (B) STAND (C) LINE (D) FIRE (E) MASTER (F) MEAL (G) TABLE (H) FEED (I) MARKET (J) CRACK

10 A 3; B 6; C 1; D 7 **(SCORE 1 POINT IF ALL ARE CORRECT; ½ POINT IF 3 ARE CORRECT)**.

11 13 **(SCORE 1 POINT)**

12 (B) **(SCORE 1 POINT)**
All the other words are made up of Roman Numerals. N is not a Roman numeral.

13 **(SCORE 1 POINT IF ALL ARE CORRECT)**
ASHTRAY ASTRAY STRAY TRAY RAY AY A

14 b, e, and h **(SCORE 1 POINT IF ALL ARE CORRECT)**.

15 140 **(SCORE 1 POINT)**
Starting with 3 in the upper half, the number in the opposite segment multiplies it by 2. the next number (7) is multiplied by 3; then by 4. and so on. Therefore, 20 is multiplied by 7 to give 140.

NOTES

In questions number 6, the volunteers did not always realize that the stripes in the tie are diagonally reversed in a mirror reflection. Numbers 7 and 15 seemed to give the greatest difficulty, though much time was lost (not always to produce a successful result) on number 9.

1 G **(SCORE 1 POINT)**
The handle is in the wrong position as compared with B and D.

2 29 **(SCORE 1 POINT)**

3 B A L E (in any order) **(SCORE 1 POINT IF ALL ARE CORRECT; ½ POINT IF 4 ARE CORRECT.)**
The words become: (A) BELATED (B) LABEL (C) BLEAT (D) EYEBALL (E) CULPABLE

4 8 **(SCORE 1 POINT)**
This is an ordinary "doubling" series, but incorrectly spaced. When correctly spaced, the answer becomes obvious: 1 2 4 8 16 32 64 128

5 (B) **(SCORE 1 POINT)**
This contains SHIN- part of the leg. All the others contain parts of the head or face: (A) HEARD contains EAR (C) CLIPPER contains LIP (D) URCHIN contains CHIN (E) DIAGNOSED contains NOSE (F) MONEYED contains EYE

6 a is 24; b is 7; c is 23; d is 7 **(SCORE 1 POINT IF ALL ARE CORRECT; ½ POINT IF 2 OR 3 ARE CORRECT)**
There are four series. Starting with the first term and taking every fourth term thereafter:

3 4 5 6 7(d)

Starting with the second term and continuing in the same way:

27 26 25 24(a)

Starting with the third term:

1 3 5 7(b)

Starting with the fourth term:

32 29 26 23(c)

7 Q **(SCORE 1 POINT)**.
The word is REQUIEM.

8 X is I, Y is Q **(SCORE 1 POINT IF BOTH ARE CORRECT; ½ POINT IS ONE IS CORRECT)**.
The Front face of each cube advances the letter on the right face by four positions in the alphabet. The top face advances the front face by three positions on the first cube, then by four positions, then by five positions, and so on. (Alternatively: increase the top faces by 7 positions at a time, the other faces by 6 positions at a time).

9 C **(SCORE 1 POINT)**.

10 x is 15, y is T z is 20 **(SCORE 1 POINT IF ALL ARE CORRECT; SCORE ½ POINT IF 2 ARE CORRECT.)**.
There are three series. Starting with the first term and taking every third term thereafter:

A L M O S – The only letter that will complete a word is T (ALMOST)—represented by y. The number that follows each letter represents the position in the alphabet of that letter. therefore, T—represented by y—should be followed by 20 (T is the 20th letter)—the value for z. Starting with the third term and taking every third term thereafter: 3 6 9 12 15 (the value for x).

11 CAR **(SCORE 1 POINT)** The words become:
(A) CARCASS   (D) CARGO
(B) CARBON   (E) CAREEN
(C) CARTON

12 669 **(SCORE 1 POINT)**
The first three license plates follow the same pattern.

The first letter gives the first digit (H is 8—its position in the alphabet).

The second letter gives the second digit by reducing its alphabetical position by 1 (G—the 7th letter—becomes 6).

The third letter gives the third digit by increasing its alphabetical position by 1

(F becomes 7, increasing its 6th position by 1).

Therefore, in the final license plate:

F gives 6 (the 6th letter)

G gives 6 (reducing the 7th letter by one)

H gives 9 (increasing the 8th letter by one).

13 x is 33; y is 117; z is 173
(SCORE 1 POINT IF ALL ARE CORRECT; ½ POINT IF 2 ARE CORRECT):

Moving down the left-hand vertical column, the numbers increase by 4, 5, and 6, and so on. 25 should be increased by 8 to give 33— the value for x.

The middle vertical column increases by 10, 11, 12, and so on. 102 should be increased by 15 to give 117—the value for y.

The right-hand vertical column increases progressively—13, 15, 17, 19, and so on. 148 should be increased by 25 to give 173—the value for z.

14 A **(SCORE 1 POINT)**.

15 **(SCORE 1 POINT IF BOTH ARE CORRECT; ½ POINT IF 4 ARE CORRECT.)**

(A) TOKEN CLERK
(B) PLATFORM
(C) TURNSTILE
(D) CONDUCTOR
(E) EXPRESS

NOTES

Definitely the most difficult test so far, this one produced very low scores by the volunteers.

Questions 6 and 10 gave examples of the "multiple series" type of question, that is, two or more series embraced in an overall series, where every second, third or fourth term has to be considered. It is good to become accustomed to this type of question since the same principle may be repeated in later tests.

Number 4 is an example of a simple series incorrectly spaced. Again, you may come across similar problems later.

Questions 4. 6. 8. and 12 gave the greatest difficulty. The time limit was extended to compensate for the test's complexity.

1 (C) **(SCORE I POINT)**.
RONDURE is a round outline or object. All the others are metrical feet:
(A) IAMBUS: a short accent followed by a long one;
(B) TROCHEE: a long accent followed by a short one;
(D) PAEON: a long accent (placed anywhere) and three short ones;
(E) SPONDEE: two long accents;
(F) DACTYL: a long accent followed by two short ones.

2 (D) **(SCORE I POINT)**
The lines are of equal length. In all the others, one line is longer (or shorter) than the other.

3 16 **(SCORE I POINT)**
Each number reverses the previous number and adds 1 to each digit. Thus, in the first two terms, 16 reversed is 61, which then changes to 72. In the final term, 50 reversed becomes 05, which in turn becomes 16 by adding one to each digit.

4 (A) 7; (B) C **(SCORE I POINT IF BOTH ARE CORRECT; ½ POINT IF ONE IS CORRECT)**

	BLACK BALL	**WHITE BALL**
1st Move	D	A
2nd Move	E	F
3rd Move	F	D
4th Move	G	B
5th Move	A	G
6th Move	B	E
7th Move	C	C

5 5 **(SCORE I POINT)**
Columns headed by an odd number add up to 30. Columns headed by an even number add up to 40. The last column adds up to 35, to which must be added 5 to bring it up to 40, as this column is headed by an even number.

6 B **(SCORE I POINT IF ALL ARE CORRECT; ½ POINT IF 4 ARE CORRECT.)**
(A) FALSETTO
(B) SOPRANO
(C) TENOR
(D) BASS
(E) ALTO

7 THEME **(SCORE I POINT)**.
This is the result of placing them together:

8 x is 11; y is 61 **(SCORE I POINT IF BOTH ARE CORRECT; ½ POINT IF ONE IS CORRECT)**.
In the first circle, the number in the top left quarter is squared and then reduced by 1 in the opposite diagonal quarter; the number in the top right quarter is cubed and then 1 added to give the number in the opposite lower quarter.

In the second circle, the same procedure is followed, except that 2 is deducted from the squared number and 2 is added to the cubed number.

Therefore, in the third circle, 3 is deducted from the square of 8 (64 becomes 61, the value for y), while 3 is added to the cube of 2 (8 becomes 11, the value for x).

9 **(SCORE I POINT IF ALL ARE CORRECT; ½ POINT IF 6 ARE CORRECT)**.
(C) MILLIMETER
(B) CENTIMETER
(E) DECIMETER
(F) METER
(A) DECAMETER
(G) HECTOMETER
(D) KILOMETER

10 (B) **(SCORE 1 POINT).**
The stripes should alternate from the edge of the flag, dark-light. In (B) they begin light-dark.

11 (B) **(SCORE 1 POINT)**
Caruso was a singer. All the others were inventors.

12 x is 9 or 24; y is also 9 or 24 **(SCORE 1 POINT IF BOTH ARE CORRECT)**
In each case, the numbers at the top are divided by 4 in the opposite quarter and 1 is added.

An alternative solution is that the numbers in the lower quarter are multiplied by 4 in their opposite quarters and 4 is deducted from the result.

13 C **(SCORE 1 POINT).**
In C there are 8 curves and 6 straight lines. In all the others there are 6 curves and 6 straight lines.

14 1 **(SCORE 1 POINT).**
The numbers reduce by 17, 34, 68, 136, 272 and so on—544 therefore reduces the previous number 545 by 1. (The terms reduce in multiples of 17.)

15 **(SCORE 1 POINT)**
In the top line, all the way through, whether using letters or numbers, they reduce by one position in each successive square.

In the bottom line, they increase by two positions, except for the last term, which reduces its position by three places from that in the previous square.

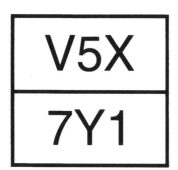

NOTES

The numerical problems seemed to give our volunteers the greatest difficulty—3, 5, and 14 particularly, though 5 was based more on logical thinking than on the numbers themselves.

Few succeeded with question number 1 and, surprisingly (now that the metric system has become more mainstream), number 9 caused a lot of problems, even though (B), (C), (F), and (D) were correctly placed.

1 55 **(SCORE 1 POINT)**

In each quarter, add the numbers in the outer ring, then those in the next ring, and then the next. In the top left quarter these totals descend:

40 39 38 37 (the single number in the center).

In the top right quarter they descend:

23 22 21 20 (the single number in the center).

In the right lower quarter they descend:

115 114 113 112 (the single number in the center). Therefore, in the lower left quarter they descend:

58 57 56 and then, obviously, 55 (x).

2 E **(SCORE 1 POINT)**

Both lines are shorter than those in the other angles.

3 a **(SCORE 1 POINT)**

The figure is rotating counter-clockwise, three faces at a time. The designs on the respective faces can be discovered by examining the figures at the top, which are in this sequence:

4 XXXVI **(SCORE 1 POINT)**

First change the Roman numerals into modern numerals:

1 3 6 10 15 21 28

It can be seen that the terms increase by:

2, 3, 4, 5, 6, and 7.

Therefore, the final number must increase the previous one by 8 (28 increases to 36, or XXXVI in Roman numerals.

5 EITHER OF THESE SOLUTIONS SCORES 1 POINT:

6 (A) **(SCORE 1 POINT)**

ESOPHAGUS is the canal from the mouth to the stomach. All the others are bones:

(B) SCAPULA—shoulder blade

(C) CLAVICLE—collarbone

(D) STERNUM—breastbone

(E) ULNA—inner bone of the forearm

(F) HUMERUS—bone of the upper arm

7 113 **(SCORE 1 POINT)**.

In each case, the number is multiplied by 6 and 1 is subtracted from the result.

8 (SCORE 1 POINT IF ALL ARE CORRECT; ½ POINT IF 8 OR 9 ARE CORRECT)

TEN	DON
MON	KEY
ORC	HARD
HID	DEN
SUN	DAY
LIGHT	BULB
CHECK	MATE
HOME	LAND
HIGH	WAY
SCHOOL	BAY

9 (A) (2); (B) (5); (C) (1); (D) (3); (E) (4) **(SCORE 1 POINT IF ALL ARE CORRECT)**.

10 (SCORE 1 POINT).

$$\frac{276}{135}$$

11 F **(SCORE 1 POINT)**

Each letter is the initial letter of the previous number, therefore: 4(FOUR) is followed by F.

12 G is of LESSER area than the others, which are all of the same area **(SCORE 1 POINT)**.

13 C **(SCORE 1 POINT)** The definite article (THE) is repeated in the second line.

14 FIR **(SCORE 1 POINT)**.

The first letter is indicated by the position of the hour hand relative to the hours—in this case 6, that is, the sixth letter (F).

The next letter is shown by the position of the second hand. Here it is on the ninth second, and the ninth letter is I.

The third letter is indicated by the position of the minute hand. As it points to the eighteenth letter in the alphabet.

15 36 **(SCORE 1 POINT)**.

NOTES

This was a difficult test for our volunteers. Questions 1, 2, 4, and 9 gained the most correct answers, but 3 and 5 might have, had the volunteers really puzzled.

In 13, it was surprisingly easy to overlook the fact that the definite article was repeated. When a book (such as this!) is in the proof stage, before being printed, it is the job of the proofreader to spot any solecisms—which creep in insidiously, however careful the typesetter has been. Proofreading is itself a very specialized job, and yet, surprisingly, it is easy enough to overlook a printing error like the one in question 13.

MASTER LEVEL

TEST 1

TIME LIMIT: 1 HOUR

1 YARBOROUGH

A hand in bridge in which all 13 cards are a nine or below is called a Yarborough, after the second earl of Yarborough (d.1897), who is said to have bet 1000 to 1 against the dealing of such a hand. What, however, are the actual odds against such a hand?

2 CRISS-CROSS

Answers run from the lower number in the direction of the next highest number, and end on that number. The next answer starts on that number and runs to the next highest number, and so on.

1	5						4	
10			13			12	7	
	17					15		
						14		
			16					
11		8				9	6	
3							2	

CLUES

1 Expressed in pictures (9)
2 Pair of eye glasses (9)
3 Tending to expand (9)
4 Bring about (8)
5 Advise again (8)
6 Small quantity (7)
7 Covered (7)
8 Slobber (5)
9 Lazily reclining (7)
10 Hot springs (7)
11 Exchanging for money (7)
12 Pleased (4)
13 Given medicine (5)
14 Beaded moisture (3)
15 Used to be (4)
16 Dash (4)
17 Incline head (3)

3 CALCULATE IT

Why does $(12570 + 0.75) \times 16 - 33 =$ An animal?

4 PALINDROME

Change the position of *one* number only to make this a palindromic sequence:

1, 4, 2, 9, 6, 1, 5, 10, 4

5 PARKED CARS

This is a true incident. See if you can figure out what actually happened.

Our country club parking lot slopes steeply from south to north, and the cars park in a vee-shape facing north (downhill), as shown in the diagram.

Recently two friends arrived to play a round of golf, and parked in spaces C and F. About two hours later, when they were halfway through their round, the club pro went onto the course to tell them that the car in space F had just rolled forward into the one in space C.

Both cars were in perfect order, had no

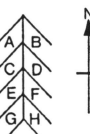

defects, and no one or nothing had pulled or pushed either car or had tampered with them in any way. What is the explanation?

6 AD NAUSEAM

What letter completes this sequence?

AEEOEEIEUE?

7 SWAP AROUND

Change the numbers to letters to find three nine-letter words:

1 2 3 4 5 6 7 8 9
2 3 1 4 5 6 7 8 9
8 9 3 1 2 4 5 6 7

8 ANAGRAM THEMES

In each set below, arrange the words in pairs so that each pair is an anagram of another word or name.

The seven words produced in (a) will have a linking theme, and the five words produced in (b) will have a linking theme. For example, if the words "DIAL" and "THAN" were in the list, they could be paired to form an anagram of "THAILAND" and the theme would be countries.

(a)

AMPLE	CREASE
CAME	MORE
CARE	RAP
CENTER	SHAKE
CHIN	THE
COIN	TO
CORD	TRY

(b)

GAIN	LAST
GRIN	LOVE
GRIP	PANS
HEAT	TRADE
HERS	TRAMP

9 NINE G-R-R-RID

Place the digits into the grid in such a way that every horizontal and vertical line when read both forwards and backwards, and also the sum of the digits of every horizontal and vertical line, can be divided by nine exactly.

1, 1, 1, 2, 2, 2, 2,
3, 3, 4, 4, 5, 5, 6
7, 7, 7, 7, 7, 7,
8, 8, 9, 9, 9.

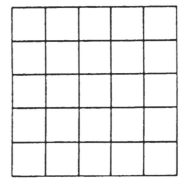

10 SPOT THE DOT

One of the dots in this circle is an intruder. Which one?

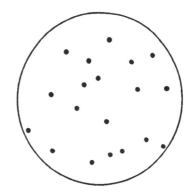

11 CROSSES

Which of these four crosses is the odd one out?

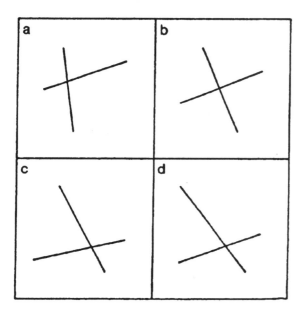

12 TARGET

Answers are all six-letter words. Pair up two sets of three letters to form the answer.

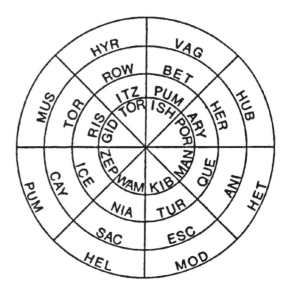

CLUES

1 SEAMEN'S CHURCH
2 ANIMATING SPIRIT
3 ALLIGATOR
4 KEPT IN THIRD PERSON'S CUSTODY
5 INSOLENT PRIDE
6 WATCH A GAME OF CARDS *KIBITZ*
7 FASHIONABLE
8 POROUS LAVA
9 RUPTURE
10 SMALL PERFUMED BAG
11 SWOLLEN
12 WHIMSICAL NOTION
13 SHELL MONEY
14 SLUGGISHNESS
15 GENTLE BREEZE
16 NECKLACE OF TWISTED METAL

13 CHILDREN

A man has nine children born at regular intervals. The sum of the square of their ages is equal to the square of his own age. What are the ages of his children?

14 CATEGORIZE

Arrange the following into groups of three:

ARQUEBUS
ATOLL
BOARD
CANAL
DOOR
FIELD
FLINTLOCK
GUN
ISLET
KEY
NOTE
STONE

15 SEQUENCE

What is the next number in this sequence, and why?

1, 4, 7, 11, 15, 18, 21, 24, 27, ?

16 CANDLES

One candle was guaranteed to burn for six hours, the other for four hours. They were both lit at the same time. After some time, one was twice as long as the other. For how long had they been burning?

17 COUNTRIES

Each horizontal row and vertical column contains the jumbled letters of a country. Find the 20 countries. Every letter on the board is used, but only once.

A	A	I	I	R	N	D	I	I	G
R	N	I	I	U	U	M	P	I	E
K	A	T	R	Y	A	U	A	E	R
K	A	A	E	Y	N	U	D	E	O
T	A	L	N	A	A	A	N	M	O
L	R	A	E	I	G	R	N	A	I
M	Y	J	L	N	I	A	A	T	T
I	N	F	A	A	P	B	J	T	A
P	M	I	N	I	C	A	A	H	S
P	P	Y	G	U	B	R	C	C	S

NOW CHECK YOUR ANSWERS AND RECORD YOUR SCORE.

1 Here is a sign of the zodiac in code:

From this you must now break this naval message received in code:

2 What is x?

A 2 D 7 x 16 V 29

3 What comes next in this series?

8 E 2 T 6 S 9
N 3 T 4 F 5 -

4 The ball in A moves clockwise, first one place, then two places, then three, and so on. When it lands on an even number the ball in B moves clockwise; when it lands on an odd number the ball in B moves counterclockwise. The ball in B also moves first one place, then two places, then three, and so on. After six moves what number will the ball in B finish on?

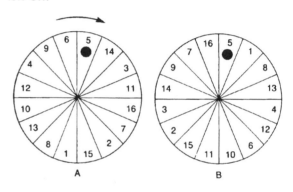

5 What are x and y in this series?

1   4   3   12   6   30   10   50   15   60   x   y

6 Which is the odd one out?

(A) GREGORY
(B) NORMAN
(C) WILLIAM

7 Which is the odd one out?

(A) TRINITY   (E) PEARL
(B) ALLEGHENY   (F) WABASH
(C) ERIE   (G) CHEYENNE
(D) DELAWARE

MASTER LEVEL **110** TEST 2

8 Assuming that you have no disabilities, where can you place your left hand where your right hand cannot touch it?

9 Arrange these into four pairs:

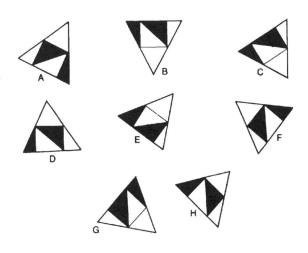

10 What should take the place of x?

2 4 5 3 4 6 7 5 6 8 9 x

11 What are x, y and z?

76 69 52 65 60 45 54 51 38
43 42 31 32 33 24 x y z

12 Form ten related pairs from these words:

GOAL TELEVISION CAR SUN STROKE
MAJOR HIGH BREAST SET KEEPER MASTER
GARAGE PICKET DRUM SERGEANT FENCE
COLOR HEAD RISE PIECE

13 Which is the greatest

(A) ¼ of 236
(B) 1/16 of 1028
(C) 1/9 of 504
(D) 1/13 of 741
(E) 1/17 of 1020

14 Which of the numbers in the bottom line should take the place of x?

121 252 x 182 255
63 128 104 255 301 336

15 What is x?

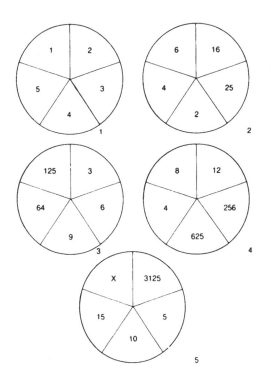

NOW CHECK YOUR ANSWERS AND RECORD YOUR SCORE.

I Give values for A, B, C, and D.

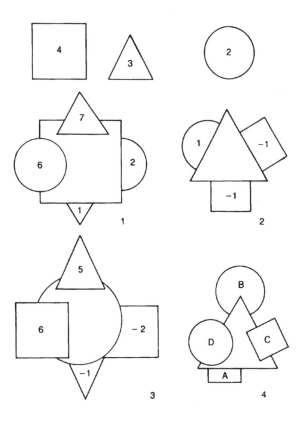

2 The two cards at the top should enable you to solve the word underneath.

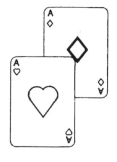

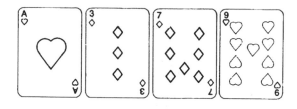

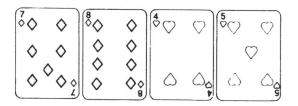

3 Which one follows No. 6?

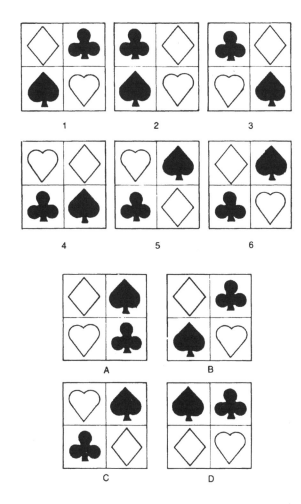

1   2   3

4   5   6

A   B

C   D

4 Which triangle is wrong?

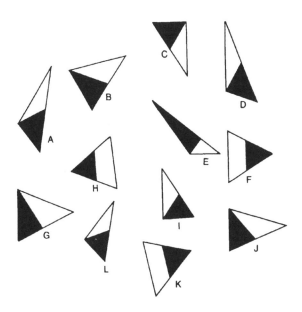

5 Pair words in the first column with words in the second column, finishing with ten connected or related pairs:

(A) OVER	(1) TEAM
(B) RUST	(2) ROOM
(C) DRAWING	(3) BELT
(D) NON	(4) LAST
(E) OUT	(5) PIN
(F) HOME	(6) SENSE
(G) SHELL	(7) STEAD
(H) HAIR	(8) FISH
(I) HEAD	(9) CAST
(J) IN	(10) BOARD

6 Subtract the sum of the prime numbers from the sum of the odd numbers (which are not prime) and add the sum of the even numbers:

3	6	7	9
11	12	14	15
16	18	19	21
27	31	33	

7

If

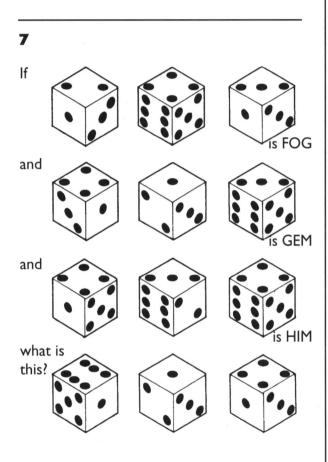

is FOG

and

is GEM

and

is HIM

what is this?

8 Three of these days have one thing in common. Which day does not share this common feature?

(A) MONDAY
(B) TUESDAY
(C) THURSDAY
(D) SATURDAY

9 Which is the odd one out?

(A) 119
(B) 21
(C) 91
(D) 77
(E) 95
(F) 105

10

If

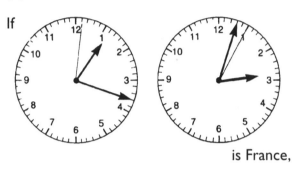

is France,

what is this?

11 If GILBERT is -1, NORMAN is 37, FRED is 23 and ARTHUR is 4, what is EDWARD?

12 What are the next two terms in this series?

36   91   21   51   82   12   42   7   –   –

13 What are A, B and C?

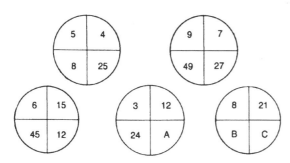

14 Which of the fractions in the bottom line should complete the series in the top line?

3.8   2⁹/₆   5⁶/₇   6.875

7¼   8.1   7⁷/₉   7¹/₉   8.375

15 If $\dfrac{P\,I\,G}{8}$ is D and $\dfrac{D\,O\,G}{13}$ is B,

what is this?

$\dfrac{C\,A\,T}{4}$

NOW CHECK YOUR ANSWERS AND RECORD YOUR SCORE.

1 Which of the figures below should occupy the vacant space?

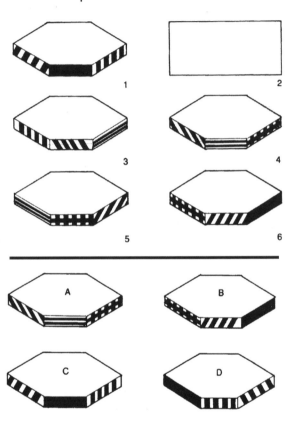

2 Which is the odd one out?

(A) BUCOLIC
(B) DIATRIBE
(C) LATIN
(D) HOURI
(E) JACK
(F) LOCUM

3 Here is a roulette wheel. When the ball stops at zero all the stakes go to the casino. The ball travels counterclockwise. At the first spin it stops at the next number. Then it misses one and stops at the next. After that each spin brings the ball one extra number along (missing two, then three, and so on). At what spin will the stakes go to the casino?

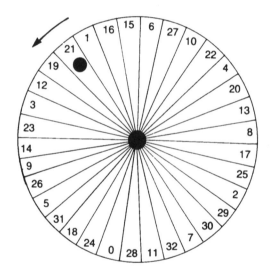

4 If CHOP is LARK, what letter completes the second word here?

FREE is DAR-

5 The top four cards should enable you to find the word represented by the bottom six cards.

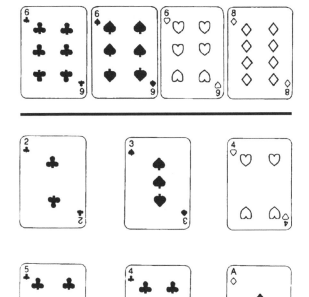

6 Which is the odd one out?

(A) BEGIN
(B) AIR
(C) DEFT
(D) WOLF
(E) BELOW
(F) BEG
(G) NOW

7 Arrange these into four pairs.

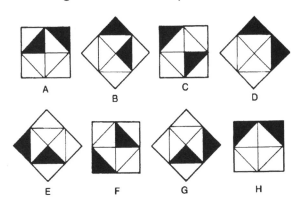

8 What goes into the empty space?

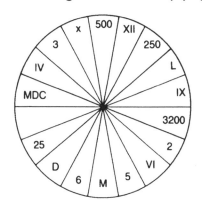

9 What comes next?

GELN-

10 Which of the cubes at the bottom should follow the two at the top?

A   B

C   D

E

11 How many seven-letter words can you make out of MALICED?

12 Complete this series, giving a value for x.

11 13 17 25 32 37 47 58 x 79

13 Who is the odd woman out?

(A) MARGUERITE
(B) PRUDENCE
(C) FELICITY
(D) BEATRICE
(E) SALLY
(F) JENNY
(G) OLIVE

14 What letter should take the place of x?

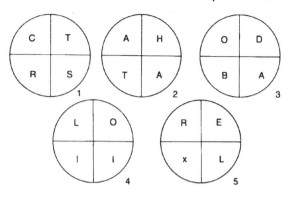

15 If A were placed on top B which of the outlines below would result?

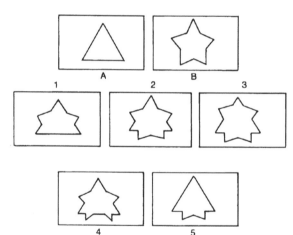

NOW CHECK YOUR ANSWERS AND RECORD YOUR SCORE.

1 Complete these words, using all the letters contained in this grammatically incorrect sentence:

HERE IS TEN FAT CATTLE
(A) –E–R–S–M–N
(B) –R–N–P–R–N–
(C) –O–T–N–N–A–

2 Which of the lower circles should take the place of number 5?

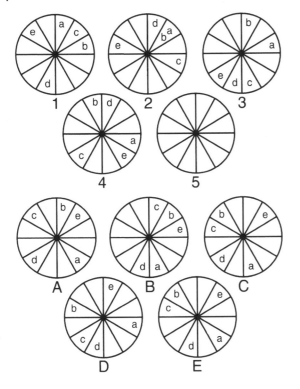

3 When a dart lands in an even number, the next throw lands it in the second odd number clockwise. When a dart lands in an odd number, the next throw lands it in the third even number clockwise from the previous throw. As you can see, the first dart has already been thrown. Four more darts are to be thrown. What will be the total score of the five darts?

4 Using the top card sequence as a key, what famous author is this?

5 What letter starts the last word?

PATCH
KINK
TEAS
—END

6 A clock shows 9:25. If it were held upside-down in front of a mirror, which of those below would be reflected?

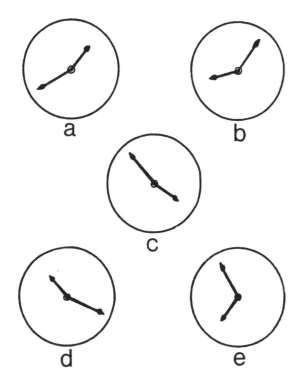

7 Which number in the bottom line should come next in the top line?

15 16 21 20 9 88 18 28 -
7 34 19 17 22 66

8 Find the words for A, B, C, D, E, F, G, and H:

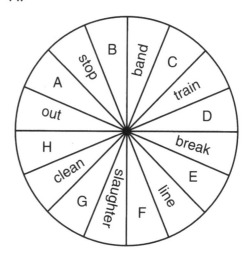

9 Which is the odd one out?

(A) USDA (B) NATO (C) NASA (D) KIWI (E) NAFTA

10 The top band rotates counter-clockwise. The middle band rotates clockwise. The bottom band rotates counter-clockwise. Each movement brings the next number into position, and there are eight numbers on each band, continuing in the same order on the hidden sides. After 7 moves, what will be the sum of the three numbers in the vertical column above A, and also the sum of the three numbers above B?

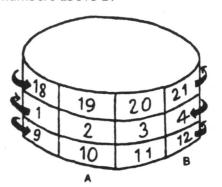

11 What comes next here?

1 8 2 7 6 4 1 2 5 2 1 -

12 What is X?

T	0
18	B
O	5
7	M
H	12
19	A
X	2

13 Which of the numbered figures at the bottom should take the places of A, B, and C?

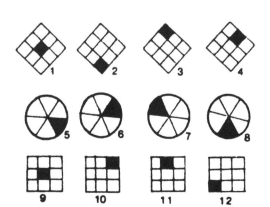

A   B   C

14 What is X?

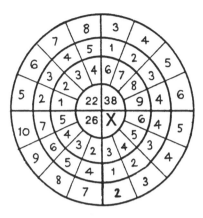

15 A advances 1 place, then 2, then 3, etc., increasing its jump by one each time. B advances 2 places, then 3, then 4 etc., increasing its jump by one each time. C advances 3 places, then 4, then 5, etc., increasing its jump by one each time. Which will be the first to reach 25 EXACTLY?

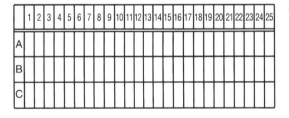

	1	2	3	4	5	6	7	8	9	10	11	12	13	14	15	16	17	18	19	20	21	22	23	24	25
A																									
B																									
C																									

NOW CHECK YOUR ANSWERS AND RECORD YOUR SCORE.

I Which of the numbered arrows belongs to X

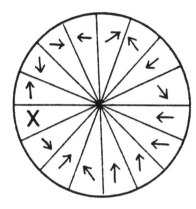

2 What goes into the last rectangle?

32	15
John

54	10
Peter

60	10
Francis

Bartholomew

3 Pinion (gear wheel) A is the driving pinion, while pinion B idles on its stub axle. The black teeth of these pinions are meshed with teeth in the outer ring. (A) After four revolutions of A in a counter-clockwise direction, where will the black tooth of pinion B be? (B) And where will it be when A has revolved clockwise through one revolution and then to where the tooth marked x meshes with the outer ring?

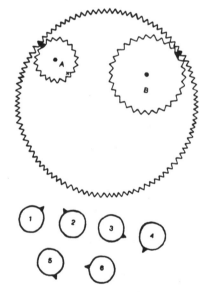

4 Which of the numbers in the bottom line should be placed under 17 in the top line?

```
2  3  4  5  6  7  8  10  11  17
7  2  17  6  13  8  3  5  4

   9  15  20  33  21  25
```

5 What comes next in this series?

I S I T P N A A
D L I I Y N —

---

6 Supply word to go into the brackets. Each word must link logically with the preceding word and the following word, e.g., tea (POT) roast

FOOD
( )
LETTER
( )
STRONG
( )
STRING
( )
BAG
( )
BOMB
( )
SHOCK
( )
LENGTH
( )
CRACK

7 Imagine that blocks x and y are removed from the arrangement below, and that the remaining shape is turned upside-down. Which of the other shapes will result?

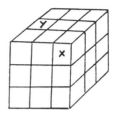

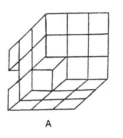

A

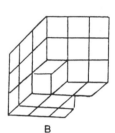

B

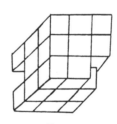

C

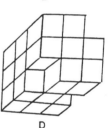

D

8 These clocks are all wrong, as indicated. If they are all correctly adjusted, which clock will show the time nearest to 12 o'clock?

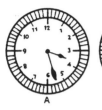  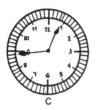

A B C

2½ hours fast   1 hour slow   1 hour 20 minutes fast

 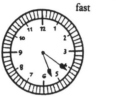

9 =3 6 6 =3 8 10 =5 6 0 =?

 = 3 6 6

= 3 8 10

= 5 6 0

= ?

10 What comes next?

2 3 4 6 1 2 2 0
1 8 4 8 1 0 –

11 Discover the key from these three problems and then break this NAVAL code.

1	2
3	4
4	9
A	B

6	8
5	2
T	E

2	1
2	2
1	3
1	1
E	S

7 ⊠ 5 9 67

 9 6

5 6 6 □

 16

 16

 1

9 1 9 1

12 Which is the odd one out?

(A) OUTSTRIP
(B) RED CURRANT
(C) SIGHING
(D) SELF-EDUCATED
(E) BIG FEET
(F) IRONMAN

13 Without using a pocket calculator, which of these investments would give the greatest interest??

(A) $1,000 at 5% simple interest for 4 years;
(B) $700 at 8% compound interest for 3 years;
(C) $900 at 7% simple interest for 3 years;
(D) $800 at 6% compound interest for 4 years. .

14 Give values for A, B, and C.

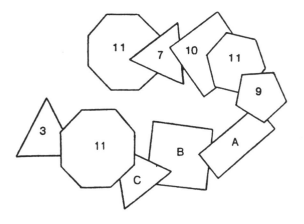

15 Write the words that fit these definitions in the corresponding rows below:

1 No lover of foreigners
2 Remove objectionable reading matter.
3 Stuffing art!
4 Still valid.
5 Not liable for duty.
6 Hydrogen and oxygen.
7 Headwear—for holding medical preparations?
8 Correct on religious doctrines.
9 It receives the mail.

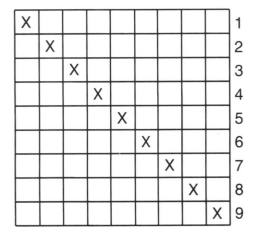

NOW CHECK YOUR ANSWERS AND RECORD YOUR SCORE.

1 What goes in the brackets?

31 (68216) 48
19 (28184) 42
36 (   ) 47

2 Can you make anything of this?

3 What goes into the vacant square?

me	ke
de	sq

ep	ua
ri	mo

bb	cr
sa	di

at	an
le	

4 Which piece completes the jigsaw puzzle?

5 What comes next?

1⅔ 2•75 3•8 4⅚ 5⁶⁄₇ 6•875

6 What letter should fill the empty space?

7 In four years I shall be five times as old as I was sixteen years ago. How old am I?

8 Which letter is in the wrong line?

AHIMOSTUVWXY
BCDEFGJKLNPQRZ

9 All these vanes move 90 degrees at a time. The longer ones rotate clockwise, first one move, then missing one and moving two (that is, through 180 degrees), then missing two and moving three, and so on. At the same time the shorter ones rotate counter-clockwise in the same way. What will be their positions after six moves?

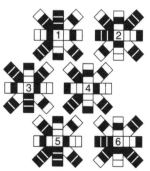

10 The black ball moves one position at a time clockwise. If it stops on an even number, the white ball moves one position clockwise. If it stops on an odd number, the white ball moves two positions counter-clockwise. On what number will both balls be in the same position?

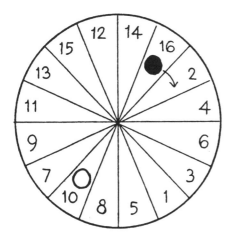

11 What comes next?

13 122 83 314 305 3 163

12 A color is concealed in each of these sentences:

(A) Temper or anger are signs of weakness.
(B) The money is for Edward.
(C) You'll find I got it elsewhere.
(D) One dancer, I see, is out of step.
(E) "I'm a gent and a lady's man," he said

13 Find a word that fits the first definition and then, by changing one letter only, a word that fits the second definition.

(A) RADIO	INDEFATIGABLE
(B) TRAIN	REMAINDER
(C) PERSON HELD FOR RANSOM	PAYMENT FOR MAIL
(D) PENITENT	DEVICE
(E) RECOIL	MOTION OF WAVE
(F) KNEAD	COMMUNICATION
(G) WEDLOCK	DEPORTMENT
(H) MODIFY STATEMENT	DEGREE OF EXCEL-LENCE
(I) NAVAL VESSEL	IDOLIZE
(J) YIELD	MOST DIFFICULT

14 Here are six clocks turned upside-down. Without turning the page right side up, which shows the nearest time to 2:25 if held in front of a mirror?

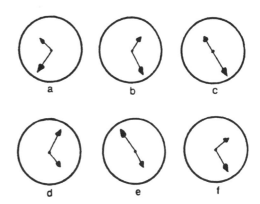

15 Complete the last line:

17 (35) 19
22 (46) 26
31 (65) 37
44 (92) 52
–   (—)   –

NOW CHECK YOUR ANSWERS AND RECORD YOUR SCORE.

1 In a pack of 52 cards there are 32 cards of nine or below. The chance that the first card dealt is one of the 32 is $^{32}\!/_{52}$, the second card $^{31}\!/_{51}$, etc. The chance of all 13 being favorable is $^{32}\!/_{52} \times ^{31}\!/_{51} \dots ^{20}\!/_{40}$ or $^{1}\!/_{1828}$. The odds were strongly in Lord Yarborough's favor.

2 1. Pictorial, 2. Lorgnette, 3. Explosive, 4. Engender, 5. Reinform, 6. Modicum, 7. Muffled, 8. Drool, 9. Lolling, 10. Geysers, 11. Selling, 12. Glad, 13. Dosed, 14. Dew, 15. Were, 16. Elan, 17. Nod.

3 Answer 604. Turn your calculator upside down and it spells hog!

4 1, 4, 9, 6, 1, 5, 10, 4, 2. Now change to Roman numerals: I, IV, IX, VI, I, V, X, IV, II.

5 When parking his car, the driver of car F had unknowingly stopped with his car touching the front bumper of a car parked in space E. Being in a hurry for the game, he forgot to put on the handbrake. When, later, the driver of car E backed out, there was no longer anything to hold car F—and it rolled forward into car C.

6 E. The preceding letters are the vowels extracted from the question!

7 Cautioned
Auctioned
Education

8 (a) Policeman (Ample Coin), Mechanic (Came Chin), Teacher (The Care), Carpenter (Rap Center), Doctor (To Cord), Secretary (Try Crease), Shoemaker (Shake More).

(b) Ptarmigan (Tramp Gain), Starling (Grin Last), Shoveler (Love Hers), Partridge (Grip Trade), Pheasant (Heat Pans).

9 52938
49617
78453
97722
21177

10 All the dots except the one on the extreme right are in orbiting groups around a central dot.

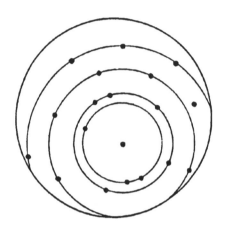

11 C. It is the only cross that will not fit snugly inside a one-inch square.

a 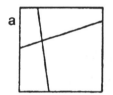 b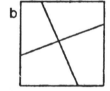

c 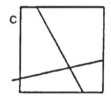 d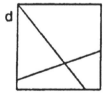

12 1. Bethel, 2. Animus, 3. Cayman, 4. Escrow, 5. Hubris, 6. Kibitz, 7. Modish, 8. Pumice, 9. Hernia, 10. Sachet, 11. Turgid, 12. Vagary, 13. Wampum, 14. Torpor, 15. Zephyr, 16. Torque.

13 Children 2 - 5 - 8 - 11 - 14 - 17 - 20 - 23 - 26
i.e. $2^2(4) + 5^2(25) + 8^2(64) + 11^2(121) + 14^2(196) + 17^2(289) + 20^2(400) + 23^2(529) + 26^2(676) = 48^2(2304).$

14 Arquebus/Field/Flintlock (All guns)
Atoll/Islet/Key (All islands)
Board/Note/Stone (All can be prefixed with KEY)
Canal/Door/Gun (All have locks).

15 73. It is spelled with 12 letters. The previous number is spelled with 11 letters, etc.

16 Three hours. After x hours,
A had burned x/6 leaving 6-x/6
B had burned x/4 leaving 4-x/4
But after x hours, A was twice as long as B.
Therefore 6-x/6 = 2(4-x)/4 Therefore x=3.

17 Lines across: India, Peru, Turkey, Kenya, Malta, Nigeria, Italy, Japan, Spain, Cyprus.

Lines down: Mali, Panama, Fiji, Niger, Iran, Cuba, Burma, Canada, Haiti, Togo.

1 A SEA ATTACK WILL START AT TEN ON WEDNESDAY **(SCORE 1 POINT)**.

The only signs of the zodiac which contain five letters are ARIES, LIBRA and VIRGO. In the coded message the first word has only one letter, corresponding with the first letter in the zodiac sign. As this cannot be L or V, it follows that the zodiac sign is ARIES. This supplies five symbols which can now be substituted in the message:

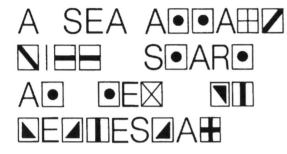

The two-letter word that starts line three begins with A, and the only possibilities are M, N or T (S has already been accounted for). Whatever this letter is, it is repeated twice in both the second word and the fifth word. In the latter case, there are no such words as SMARM or SNARN, so that only leaves T. (Also, T is probably the most commonly used consonant, and is featured no fewer than six times in the message.)

So the fifth word is START and the sixth word is AT. Also, the third word, as we now know, starts with ATTA — and (remember we are dealing with a naval message) ATTACK is a reasonable assumption. In fact, the only six-letter words which start this way are ATTACH, ATTACK and ATTAIN. It cannot be ATTAIN, because I has already been accounted for. The fourth word ends with a double letter: –I––. This double letter cannot be A, B, C, D, G, H, J, K, M, N, O, P, Q, R, T, U, V, W, X, Y or Z, and must be F or L. As the only words ending in FF are BIFF, JIFF and TIFF — none of which is likely and the T is already accounted for—it is more probable that it ends in LL: –ILL. It is clearly BILL, DILL, FILL, GILL, HILL, KILL, MILL, PILL or WILL, and the most likely choices are KILL or WILL. If it is KILL, it means that the last word starts with KE, but with the letters already fitted, (and using reasonable deduction) the choice is almost bound to be WE, and the full word itself, WEDNESDAY, should fall into place from WE-N (N has already been deduced from the seventh word: TE-) ES-A-(W was deduced

from WILL earlier). From the context of what has now been solved it should be clear which symbols represent O (as in the eighth word) and D and Y (as in the last word).

You may have decoded this message using different methods, but the important thing is to arrive at the correct solution, whether through inspired guessing or clever deduction.

2 11 **(SCORE 1 POINT)**.

Substituting numbers for letters, according to the position in the alphabet of the letters, the series becomes:

1   2   4   7   x   16   22   29

The numbers are increasing by 1, 2, 3, etc. So x will be 7 + 4.

3 F **(SCORE 1 POINT)**.

Each letter is the initial letter of the letter preceding it: 8 (Eight), 2 (Two), etc., and so 5 (Five).

4 9 **(SCORE 1 POINT)**.

The moves are as follows:

	A	B
1st move	14	1
2nd move	11	16
3rd move	2	8
4th move	13	7
5th move	6	13
6th move	7	9

5 x is 21; y is 84 **(SCORE 1 POINT IF BOTH ARE CORRECT; ½ IF ONE)**.

There are two series here. Starting with the first term and proceeding alternately:

1   3   6   10   15

The terms increase by 2, 3, 4 and 5. Therefore 15 must be increased by 6, making x 21.

In the second series, preceding ODD numbers are multiplied by 4 and preceding EVEN numbers are multiplied by 5, which gives:

4	(1×4)
12	(3×4)
30	(6×5)
50	(10×5)
60	(15×4)

So y is 21×4.

6 (C) **(SCORE 1 POINT).**
Although they are all boys' names, (A) and (B) also contain other boys' names in reverse: ROGER and RON.

7 (C) **(SCORE 1 POINT).**
Except for (C), these are all names of major North American Rivers. (C) Erie is a Great Lake.

8 On your right elbow **(SCORE 1 POINT).**
This is the only place which is completely out of reach of the right hand.

9 AF; BC; DH; EG **(SCORE 1 POINT IF ALL ARE CORRECT).**

10 7 **(SCORE 1 POINT).**
Each pair of digits is reversed and has 1 added to each digit to become the next pair. Thus 24, reversed and with 1 added to 2 and 1 added to 4, becomes 53, 53 becomes 46, 46 becomes 75, 75 becomes 68. Therefore 68 must become 97.

11 x is 21; y is 24; z is 17 **(SCORE 1 POINT IF ALL ARE CORRECT; ½ IF 2).**
There are three separate series here. Starting with the first term and taking every third term thereafter:

76   65   54   43   32

As they reduce by 11 each time, the next term, x, must be 21.

From the second term and proceeding in the same way, we get:

69   60   51   42   33

These reduce by 9 each time, so the next term, y, is 24.
From the third term, we get:

52   45   38   31   24

As these reduce by 7 each time, the next term, z, is 17.

12 **(SCORE 1 POINT IF ALL ARE CORRECT; ½ IF 8 OR 9.)**
GOAL KEEPER; PICKET FENCE; CAR GARAGE; SUN SET; HIGH RISE; COLOR TELEVISION; SERGEANT MAJOR; DRUM HEAD; MASTER PIECE; BREAST STROKE

13 (B) **(SCORE 1 POINT).**
(A) 59
(B) 64¼
(C) 56
(D) 57
(E) 60

14 104 **(SCORE 1 POINT).**
121 is divisible by 11;
252 is divisible by 12;
104 (x) is divisible by 13;
182 is divisible by 14;
255 is divisible by 15.

15 1024 **(SCORE 1 POINT).**
Start at 1 in the first circle and move clockwise throughout, missing two segments each time:

1   2   3   4   5

The numbers increase by 1 each time.
Starting at 2 in the first circle:

2   4   6   8   10

The numbers increase by 2 each time.
Starting at 3 in the first circle:

3   6   9   12   15

The numbers increase by three each time.
Starting at 4 in the first circle:

4   16   64   256   1024   (x)

The numbers were multiplied by 4 each time.
Starting at 5 in the first circle:

5   25   125   625   3125

The numbers were multiplied by 5 each time.

NOTES

4, 5, 11 and 15 caused the greatest difficulty and took the longest time. Surprisingly, I did not present the difficulty nor wasted the time expected. It was either solved comparatively quickly or not solved at all. Once it was realized that the zodiac sign had to be ARIES, the rest seemed to fall into place without much complication.

Again, 3 was either surprisingly difficult or surprisingly easy. If it was realized quickly that the letters were the initials of the numbers, the answer came almost immediately; if not, there was simply nothing to go on, as there was no noticeable regularity of any kind in the series.

The time limit was generous enough to allow for the amount of working-out involved with 1, 4 and 12.

1 A is -1; B is 1; C is 7; D is 5 (SCORE 1 POINT IF ALL ARE CORRECT; ½ IF 3).

We know that a square is worth 4 points, a triangle 3 points and a circle 2 points.

A figure lying ABOVE another adds its value to that of the one below. A figure lying BENEATH another deducts its value from the one above. So, in the first diagram:

The top triangle (3) adds its value to the square beneath it (4) and is worth 7; the circle on the left (2) adds its value to the square beneath it (4) and is worth 6; the bottom triangle subtracts its value (3) from that of the square (4) and is worth 1; the circle on the right subtracts its value (2) from that of the square (4) and is worth 2.

Thus in the last diagram:
square A is worth -1 (3 - 4);
circle B is worth 1 (3 - 2)
square C is worth 7 (4 + 3)
circle D is worth 5 (3 + 2)

2 APTITUDE (SCORE 1 POINT).

Another problem based on the 26 letters of the alphabet corresponding with the 26 cards in two suits. Here hearts represent A to M (ace to king); diamonds represent N to Z (ace to king).

Ace of hearts	1st letter	A
3 of diamonds	16th letter	P
7 of diamonds	20th letter	T
9 of hearts	9th letter	I
7 of diamonds	20th letter	T
8 of diamonds	21st letter	U
4 of hearts	4th letter	D
5 of hearts	5th letter	E

3 B (SCORE 1 POINT).

In square 2 the top two suits in square 1 are transposed. In square 3 the bottom two suits in square 2 are transposed. In square 4 the left vertical column in square 3 is transposed. In square 5 the right vertical column in square 4 is transposed. In square 6 the top left has been transposed with the bottom right in square 5. Therefore, in the next square the top right will be transposed with the bottom left in square 6.

4 E (SCORE 1 POINT).

There are four different types of triangle here:

equilateral (all sides equal)

isosceles (two sides equal)

right-angled (one right angle)

scalene (all sides unequal)

Each is shaded according to its type, the scalene triangle being shaded like this:

In E, however, it is shaded like this:

5 (A) (9); (B) (3); (C) (10); (D) (6); (E) (4); (F) (1); (G) (8); (H) (5); (I) (2); (J) (7) (SCORE 1 POINT IF ALL ARE CORRECT; ½ IF 8 OR 9). You may score 1 point if you have used other combinations of words—but only if you have all ten correct.

6 100 (SCORE 1 POINT).

7 ICE (SCORE 1 POINT).

In the first row the spots on each cube are added and given letters equal to their position in the alphabet:
6 (F) 15 (O) 7 (G)
In the second row 1 is deducted from the total of the spots on each cube. In the third row 2 is deducted from each total. In the last row 3 is deducted from each total:
12-3=9 (I)
6-3=3 (C)
8-3=5 (E)

8 (A) (SCORE 1 POINT).

The others contain two consecutive letters of the alphabet:
(B) **TU**esday
(C) thu**RS**day
(D) sa**TU**rday

9 (E) (SCORE 1 POINT).

All the other numbers are divisible by 7.

10 CANADA (SCORE 1 POINT).

The hour hand of the first clock is at 6; the sixth letter of the alphabet is F. The minute hand is at 18: R. The second hand is at 1: A. On the second clock, the hour hand is at 14: N. The minute hand is at 3: C. The second hand is at 5: E. Follow the same principle for the other to clocks and you get CANADA.

11 -27 (SCORE 1 POINT).

Substitute numbers for letters according to their alphabetical position. Add the value of the first and second letters, subtract the third, add the next, then subtract, and so on:

E(5)+D(4)-W(23)+A(1)-R(18)+D(4)

5+4-23+1-18+4=-27

12 3 and 0 (SCORE 1 POINT IF BOTH ARE CORRECT).

The series must be spaced correctly:

3   6   9   12   15   18   21   24   27

The terms increase by 3 throughout, so 30 is next.

13 A is 9; B is 63; C is 16 (SCORE 1 POINT IF ALL ARE CORRECT).

Prime numbers are squared in the opposite quarter; even numbers are doubled in the opposite quarter; odd numbers are tripled in the opposite quarter.

14 $7\frac{1}{9}$ (SCORE 1 POINT).

Convert all the fractions in the top line into improper fractions:

$3\frac{4}{5}$ $4\frac{5}{6}$ $5\frac{6}{7}$ $6\frac{7}{8}$

This establishes the pattern:

345   456   567   678

So the final fraction must represent 789, which is $7\frac{1}{9}$.

15 F (SCORE 1 POINT).

If each letter has a value according to its position in the alphabet, the total of each word is as follows:
P I G ... 32
D O G ... 26
C A T ... 24
32(PIG)÷8=4 — that is, D (the 4th letter)
26(DOG)÷13=2—that is, B (the 2nd letter)
24 (CAT)÷4=6—that is, F (the 6th letter)

NOTES

If you have followed these tests and explanations through, 2 should not have given too much trouble, as it is based on a question-type used before. 5, 7, 10 and 11 were the most time-consuming.

The incorrectly spaced series in 12 (the answer becomes very obvious when it is correctly spaced) should also have not been too troublesome to ardent followers of these tests. Previously I have advised you to keep a look-out for series which are incorrectly spaced.

In 8 the strange coincidence of two consecutive letters in alphabetical order eluded many—probably because it was so obvious!

11 was very difficult, but the clue lay in the minus value given for GILBERT, which should have indicated that there had to be deductions as well as additions.

TEST 4 ANSWERS

1 D **(SCORE 1 POINT).**
The figure is rotating clockwise.

2 (C) **(SCORE 1 POINT).**
The first and last letters of all the others are consecutive in the alphabet.
(A) BucoliC
(B) DiatribE
(C) Hourl
(D) JacK
(E) LocuM

3 The 9th spin **(SCORE 1 POINT).**
1st spin 19
2nd spin 3
3rd spin 9
4th spin 18
5th spin 32
6th spin 17
7th spin 27
8th spin 3
9th spin . . . . ZERO

4 K **(SCORE 1 POI9NT).**
Give each letter a value according to its position in the alphabet. The total value of the letters in CHOP (42) is the same as that in LARK (42). The total value of the letters in FREE is 34. The total value of the letters in DAR is 23, which means that the last letter must have the value of 11 to bring it up to 34. The 11th letter of the alphabet is K.

5 BIPEDS **(SCORE 1 POINT).**
Another problem based on the 26 letters of the alphabet corresponding with certain cards. Here clubs represent A to F (ace to 6); spades represent G to L (ace to 6); hearts represent M to R (ace to 6); diamonds represent S to Z (ace to 8). Therefore:

2 of clubs	B	(2nd letter)
3 of spades	I	(9th letter)
4 of hearts	P	(16th letter)
5 of clubs	E	(5th letter)
4 of clubs	D	(4th letter)
Ace of diamonds	S	(19th letter)

6 (D) **(SCORE 1 POINT).**
All the other words contain letters in alphabetical order.

7 AE; BG; CF; DH **(SCORE 1 POINT IF ALL ARE CORRECT).**

8 18 **(SCORE 1 POINT).**
Each modern number in any one segment has a number in Roman numerals in its opposite segment. Starting with MDC (1600), this is doubled in the opposite segment to give 3200. Moving clockwise, IV is halved, to give 2 in the opposite segment. This doubling and halving continues, so by the time we get to IX (9), this must be doubled in the opposite segment to give 18, expressed in modern digits.

9 D **(SCORE 1 POINT).**
These are the initial letters of the first five books of the Bible (the Pentateuch): Genesis, Exodus, Leviticus, Numbers, followed by Deuteronomy.

10 B **(SCORE 1 POINT).**
Examination of the top cubes reveals that they are rotating forwards (confirmed by the changed positions of the two spots on the side). As far as the facing side is concerned, B, C, D or E could be correct, but only in B have the two spots changed their positions in keeping with the forward rotation.

11 Four **(SCORE 1 POINT IF ALL ARE CORRECT).**
DECLAIM
CLAIMED
MEDICAL
DECIMAL

12 71 **(SCORE 1 POINT).**
Each number is increased by adding the total of its digits to the number itself. So, 11 (1+1=2) becomes 13, 13 (1+3=4) becomes 17, etc.
Following this procedure, 58 (5+8=13) becomes 71.

13 (D) **(SCORE I POINT).**

They are all women's names, but all except (D) are also nouns:

(A) MARGUERITE - the ox-eye daisy
(B) PRUDENCE - wisdom
(C) FELICITY - happiness
(E) SALLY - a going-forth
(F) JENNY - female donkey
(G) OLIVE - fruit

14 ○ **(SCORE I POINT).**

The circles contain four five-lettered words. Starting with C in the first circle, notice how the following letters move one place clockwise in each successive circle:

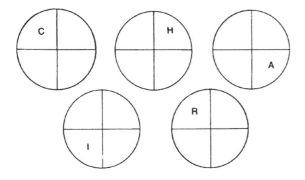

Starting with T in the first circle and proceeding in the same way, we get:

T A B L E

Starting with S in the first circle, we get:

S T O O L

Starting with R in the first circle, we get:

R A D I-

Obviously, the only possible word that falls into the household context of the other words is RADIO, so the missing letter is O.

15 2 **(SCORE I POINT).**

A relatively easy test (to give your brain a rest after the hard mental work you have done so far!).

5 should have given little difficulty if you have followed the reasoning on previous problems of this nature. Many of our volunteers failed to get all four words in 11, the omission usually being DECLAIM. 3 and 14 gave the greatest difficulty, but all in all the scores were somewhat higher than in the previous tests in this section.

1 (SCORE 1 POINT IF ALL ARE CORRECT.)
(A) REFRESHMENT
(B) TRANSPARENT
(C) CONTINENTAL

2 E (SCORE 1 POINT)
a moves one place at a time clockwise; b moves one place at a time counter-clockwise; c moves two places at a time clockwise; d moves to and from opposite segments; e moves counter-clockwise, first one place, then two, then three, and so on.

3 68 (SCORE 1 POINT)
1st throw...18
2nd throw...15
3rd throw...8
4th throw...9
5th throw...18 (again)
Total 68

4 MARK TWAIN (SCORE 1 POINT)
The four cards at the top indicate the first 23 letters of the alphabet:
Ace of hearts up to the 5...1-5 or A to E
Ace of Clubs up to the 4...6-9, F to I
Ace of spades up to the 7...10-16, or J to P
Ace of diamonds up to the 7...17-23, or Q to W

5 V (SCORE 1 POINT)
Giving each letter a value according to its position in the alphabet, each word must have a total letter-value of 45. The three letters of the unfinished word have a total of 23, which must be increased to 45 with the addition of 22—that is, the 22nd letter of the alphabet—V.

6 b (SCORE 1 POINT)

7 66 (SCORE 1 POINT).
The numbers at the top are divisible by 3 and 4 alternately. The only number in the bottom line that is divisible by 3 is 66.

8 (SCORE 1 POINT IF ALL CORRECT; ½ POINT IF 7 ARE CORRECT.)
The position of the letters from A to H indicates that the word are considered in a clockwise direction. Starting with OUT, and reading clockwise:
out
(A) BACK
stop
(B) WATCH
band
(C) WAGON
train
(D) STATION
break
(E) FRONT
line
(F) MAN
slaughter
(G) HOUSE
clean
(H) CUT
out

9 D (SCORE 1 POINT).
Apart from KIWI, which is a non-flying bird, a fruit, and also a slang term for a non-flying member of the New Zealand Air Force, the other are all acronyms (words formed from the initial letters of other words):
(A) USDA United States Department of Agriculture
(B) NATO North Atlantic Treaty Organization
(C) NASA National Aeronautic and Space Administration
(E) NAFTA North American Free Trade Agreement

10 A 32; B 38 (SCORE 1 POINT IF BOTH ARE CORRECT; ½ POINT IF 1 IS CORRECT).

	A	B
1st Move	18	29
	3	5
	9	11
2nd Move	25	19
	4	6
	16	19
3rd Move	24	18
	5	7
	15	9
4th Move	23	25
	6	8
	14	16

5th Move	22	24
	7	1
	13	15
6th Move	21	23
	8	2
	12	14
7th Move	20	22
	1	3
	11	13
Total	32	38

11 6 (SCORE 1 POINT)

Correcting the spacing, the series becomes:
1 8 27 64 125 21 –
That is: the cubes of: 1, 2, 3, 4, 5, 6. the cube of 6 is 216, which means that 6 must follow 21

12 R (SCORE 1 POINT)

Substituting numbers for letters according to their position in the alphabet, each horizontal row adds up to 20. Therefore, X must be 18, as it is paired with 2, and R is the 18th letter.

13 A 5; B 2; C 12 (SCORE 1 POINT IF ALL ARE CORRECT; ½ POINT IF 2 ARE CORRECT).

Consider the movements of the black section in each figure. It goes diagonally across the square from bottom left to top right and then back again:

In the circle, it moves two segments at a time in a clockwise direction:

In the diamond it moves alternately from top to bottom:

14 22 (SCORE 1 POINT).

In each quarter of the circle: add the numbers in the outer ring; subtract the sum of the numbers in the next ring; add the sum of the number in the next ring to give the number that goes into the inner section. So:

the sum of 2, 3, 4, and 5	14
subtract the sum of 1, 2, 3, and 4	10
	4
add the sum of 3, 4, 5, and 6	18
	22

15 C (SCORE 1 POINT)

The relative positions are shown below:

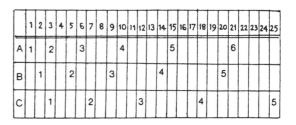

NOTES

Questions 4, 7, 8, 10, and 13 were probably the most difficult. regarding 4 (since you may come across other problems of this kind), it is worth bearing in mind the coincidence that there are 52 cards in a pack—or 26 in half a pack (the equivalent of two suits)—and 26 letters in the alphabet. Be aware of this fact, as we may use this tactic again in the future. I was amused to witness the antics of some volunteers who were trying to figure out the answer to number 6. Holding the page upside-down, and even holding it up to the light and trying to see through it from the reverse side were common strategies. As for number 11, you were advised previously to keep an eye open for series—such as this—which were incorrectly spaced. I hope that you benefited from past experience.

1 (SCORE 1 POINT). Start with the arrow above X. In the opposite segment it is turned 90 degrees counter-clockwise. the next is turned 90 degrees clockwise. this alternating rotation is continued. Therefore, in the opposite segment to X, the arrow must be turned 90 degrees clockwise (number 4).

2 (SCORE 1 POINT) 96 36 Add the letter-values of the consonants according to their position in the alphabet and enter the total in the left-hand side.

Then enter the total of the value of the vowels in the right-hand side:
B 2; R 18; T 20; H 8; L 12;
M 13; W 23...Total 96
A 1; O 15; O 15 O E 5...Total 36

3 (SCORE 1 POINT IF BOTH ARE CORRECT; ½ POINT IF 1 IS CORRECT.) (A) 5; (B) 1
There are 20 teeth on A and 30 on B
The large annular ring will rotate in the same direction as the driving pinion.

(A) After 4 revolutions of A the outer ring will rotate in the same direction as the driving pinion. (A) After 4 revolutions of A the outer ring will rotate counter-clockwise through 80 teeth, causing the idling pinion to rotate through 2 revolutions (60 teeth) and an additional 20 teeth.

(B) The driving pinion will rotate through 30 teeth—the same number as on the idling pinion, which will bring the black tooth on B to where it was originally(1).

4 20 **(SCORE 1 POINT)** Even numbers have prime numbers beneath them. Prime numbers have even numbers beneath them. 17 is a prime number, and must have an even number beneath it.

The only even number in the third line is 20.

5 A **(SCORE 1 POINT)** There are three separate series. Starting with the first letter and taking every third letter thereafter:
ITALY
Starting with the second letter and taking every third letter thereafter:
SPAIN
From the third letter:
INDIA

6 (SCORE 1 POINT IF ALL ARE CORRECT; ½ POINT IF 6 OR 7 ARE CORRECT.)
food
CHAIN
letter
HEAD
strong
BOX
string
BEAN
bag
PIPE
bomb
SHELL
shock
WAVE
length
WISE
crack

7 B **(SCORE 1 POINT).** Removing blocks x and y leaves the following: Turned upside-down, this corresponds with B.

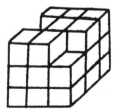

8 D **(SCORE 1 POINT).**

When adjusted, the clocks show the following times:
A from 3:27 to 12:57
B from 11:13 to 12:13
C from 1:44 to 12:24
D from 10:32 to 11:52
E from 5:21 to 12:19

9 2 4 12 **(SCORE 1 POINT IF ALL ARE CORRECT; ½ POINT IF 2 ARE CORRECT).**

The first number equals the number of CENTER spots.

The second number is the total of the spots that surround the center spots.

The third number is the total of the remaining spots.

10 0 **(SCORE 1 POINT).**

There are three separate series, though digits representing tens are not placed adjacent to the units. For example, 12 is shown as 1 2. Starting with the first term, each third term thereafter multiplies the previous term by 3:

2—6——18——

Starting with the second term, each third term thereafter multiplies the previous term by 4:

-3—12——48—-

Starting with the third term, each third term thereafter multiplies the previous term by 5:

—4—-20——100.

The final term (to complete 100) is 0.

11 SUBMARINES HAVE BEEN SIGHTED IN THE NORTH ATLANTIC **(SCORE 1 POINT)**

From the sum on the right it is obvious that S is 7. It must be decided whether the middle one is an addition or a subtraction, but it cannot be an addition, because it would then have a three-digit answer. As it must be a subtraction, E must be 6 and T must be 1.

The left-hand problem must be an addition, so B must be 5 and A must be 9.

Substituting these letters in the code:

S – B – A – – – E – S
– A – E
BEE –
S – – –TE –
– –T – E
– – –T –
AT – A –T – –

Certain words now become apparent, such as SUBMARINES and ATLANTIC.

The third word (4 letters) and the sixth word (3 letters) are worth considering:

BEE –   T – E

The first must be BEER or BEEN, and the second must be THE TIE or TOE. As it is unlikely that the seventh word ends in TI or TO, but could probably end in TH, it is reasonable to assume that the sixth word is THE. By substituting H wherever it occurs:

S – B – A – – NESHA – EBEENS– – HTE– – NTHEN– –THAT – ANT– –

Even if by now the other words do not become apparent, the last word should be obvious:

AT – ANT– –

(remembering that it is a naval code).

This will supply L, I, and C, and the rest should fall into place.

12 (C) **(SCORE 1 POINT IF BOTH ARE CORRECT)** SIGHING contains three letters in alphabetical order—GHI.

All the others contain three letter in reverse alphabetical order:

(A) oUTStrip
(B) rED-Currant
(C) selF-EDucated
(E) biG FEet
(F) irONMan

13 (D) **(SCORE 1 POINT).**
(A) would show $200 interest
(B) would show $182 interest
(C) would show $189 interest
(D) would show $210 interest

14 A is 8; B is 7; C is 11 **(SCORE 1 POINT IF ALL ARE CORRECT).**

Starting at the octagon (11) at the top left and moving clockwise, add the number of sides to the figure to the number of sides on its adjacent figure. the figure before A is a pentagon (5 sides) and has a value of 9 (5 added to A, which is a square). Therefore, A (4 sides) is added to C (a triangle), giving B a value of 7. C (3 sides) is added to the next figure (an octagon), giving C a value of 11.

15 (SCORE 1 POINT IF ALL ARE CORRECT; ½ POINT IF 7 OR 8 ARE CORRECT).

1 XENOPHOBE
2 EXPURGATE
3 TAXIDERMY
4 UNEXPIRED
5 UNTAXABLE
6 HYDROXIDE
7 PILLBOXES
8 ORTHODOXY
9 LETTERBOX

NOTES

Question number 5 was another example of a "multiple" series, in which every third factor was taken, instead of every consecutive one. Your previous experience of this type of series may have helped you out. A great deal of time had to be spent on numbers 8, 11, and 13. 13, of course, could have been solved much faster with the aid of a calculator. Incidentally, the amounts given in the answer ignore decimal fractions. Hardly anybody succeeded with number 9—not surprising, since there was little beyond sheer inspiration to guide you on your way. In case I am accused—in number 11—of not giving a totally unambiguous solution to every coded letter, I can only claim that, since it was a naval code, S – B – A – – N – ES and AT – ANT – – could be reasonably be assumed to lead to SUBMARINES and ATLANTIC. The seventh word, (NORTH), with only – – – TH to go on, could not have been south, as S had already been accounted for. Finally, HA – E (following a plural word) could be taken as HAVE.

TEST 7 ANSWERS

1 681214 **(SCORE 1 POINT)**

The left-hand digit of the number on the left of the brackets is doubled to give the first digit inside the brackets.

The left-hand digit of the number on the right of the brackets is doubled to give the second digit inside the brackets.

The right-hand digit of the number on the left of the brackets is doubled to give the second number inside the brackets.

The right-hand digit of the number on the right of the brackets is doubled to give the next number inside the brackets.

2 THIS **(SCORE 1 POINT)**

Move the top pieces left and down. Move the bottom pieces to the right and up.

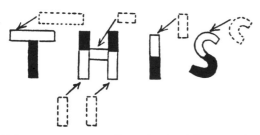

3 ke **(SCORE 1 POINT)** From the top left quarter in the first square, move one position counter-clockwise throughout:

me   ri   di   an

Use the same procedure in the other quarters:

de   mo   cr   at
sq   ua   bb   le
ke   ep   sa   ke

4 B **(SCORE 1 POINT)**

5 **(SCORE 1 POINT)**

Express all the terms as uneven fractions:

1⅔ 2¾ 3⅘ 5⁶⁄₇ 6⅞

Now it is obvious that the terms progress like this:

123 234 345 456 567 678 —

and that the final term must be 789, expressed as an uneven fraction as in the examples:

7⁸⁄₉

6 L **(SCORE 1 POINT)**

Starting from C, read the opposite letter (A) and then return to the opposite side, moving clockwise to the next position (T). This gives CAT.

Following this procedure:

DOG PIG SOW BUL(L)

Below is shown the order in which the segments are considered:

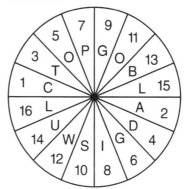

7 21 **(SCORE 1 POINT)** If x represents age, then x+4=5(x-16).

Therefore:

x+4=5x-80, from which: 84=4x, so x=21.

8 S **(SCORE 1 POINT)**. All the letters in the top line except S will read the same if reflected in a mirror.

S should be in the bottom line, in which every letter would read backwards if reflected in a mirror.

9 5 **(SCORE 1 POINT)**.

CHALLENGING LEVEL **141** TEST 7 ANSWERS

10 15 **(SCORE 1 POINT)**.

The balls move as follows:

BLACK BALL	WHITE BALL
2	7
4	9
6	11
3	7
1	8
5	1
8	5
10	8
7	1
9	6
11	2
13	14
15	15

11 0 **(SCORE 1 POINT)**

Correctly spaced, the series becomes:

1 31 2 28 3 31 4 30 5 31 6 3 —

the series is based on the days and months of the year—the month followed by the number of days. June has 30 days, so the final term should be 30

12 **(SCORE 1 POINT IF ALL ARE CORRECT)**
(A) ORANGE
(B) RED
(C) INDIGO
(D) CERISE
(E) MAGENTA

13 **(SCORE 1 POINT IF ALL ARE CORRECT; ½POINT IF 8 OR 9 ARE CORRECT)**

(A) WIRELESS	TIRELESS
(B) RETINUE	RESIDUE
(C) HOSTAGE	POSTAGE
(D) CONTRITE	CONTRIVE
(E) BACKLASH	BACKWASH
(F) MASSAGE	MESSAGE
(G) MARRIAGE	CARRIAGE
(H) QUALIFY	QUALITY
(I) WARSHIP	WORSHIP
(J) HARVEST	HARDEST

14 d **(SCORE 1 POINT)**

15 **(SCORE 1 POINT)**

The numbers on each side of the brackets alternately increase by 2, 3, 4, 5, 6, 7, 8 (and then 9 and 10). to discover the number inside the brackets: double the number on the left and add 1, then 2, then 3, then 4, and finally 5 (122 plus 5-127)

NOTES

The volunteers experienced greatest difficulty with 3, 6, 9, and 11, though, in the case of 11, they were warned to look out for series which are incorrectly spaced. When the series is spaced correctly, the relationship between the months and days becomes apparent. The important clue to solving number 3 was the fact that q is always followed by u. This leads to the fact that SQ in square 1 must be followed by UA in the next square. This combination may have pointed to the order in which all the letters were positioned. In the Answers, I offer an algebraic solution to number 7, though it can be solved by trial and error. Unless you are lucky, algebra offers the quickest solution. The most time-consuming problems were 3, 9, 13, and (in particular) 10.

COMPREHENSIVE SUPERTESTS

TEST 1

TIME LIMIT: 55 MINUTES

1 ODD ONE OUT

Which is the odd one out and why?

CHIS   PERL

DENC   FRAP

PORL   SPAD

2 TILES

A two-and-a-half-inch square card is thrown at random onto a tiled floor. What are the odds against its falling not touching a line? You should assume that the pattern repeats over a large area.

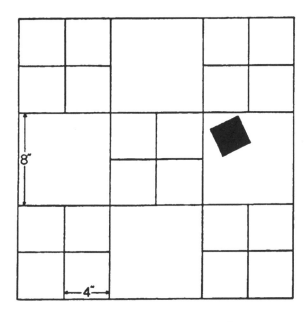

3 AMICABLE NUMBERS

These are rare numbers. They are pairs of numbers in which the sum of the factors of one is equal to the other, and vice versa. What are the two numbers in the first pair? They are both under 300.

?	?
1184	1210
5020	5564
6232	6368
10744	10856
17926	18416
9437056	9363584

NOW CHECK YOUR ANSWERS AND RECORD YOUR SCORE.

TEST 2

TIME LIMIT: 1 HOUR 30 MINUTES

1 LETTERS

(a) What letters complete these sequences?

(i) M, V, E, M, J, S, U, N, ?

(ii) C, D, I, L, M, V, ?

(iii) P, W, E, L, G, A, ?

(b) What is the next letter in this sequence?

O, T, F, S, N, E, T, F, S, N, T, T, ?

(c) What vowels complete these sequences?

(i) E, OAE, EO, EE, UE, IIO, ?

(ii) UA, OA, UEA, EEA, UA, IA, ?

(d) Should the letter K go above or below the line?

A   E F   H I
_____
   B C D   G   J

(e)* Fill in the missing letters.

2 NUMBERS

(a) Work out the missing numbers.

(i) 4, 9, 25, 49, 121, 169, 289, 361, ?, ?, 961

(ii) 97376, 7938, 1512, ?

(iii) 1, 4, 27, 256, ?

(iv) 33278, 9436, 4278, 2996, ?

(v) 22196, 4294, 988, ?

(b) Consider the number 7731.

Now continue the sequence: 153, 193, 197, 353, 413, 419, 793, 797, 813, 819, ?, ?

(c) Find the reason for arranging these numbers into groups of three. 127, 196, 361, 414, 428, 533, 565, 566, 693, 761, 775, 961.

(d) Work out the missing number.

3 WORDS

(a) What do these words have in common?

STUDIO, CALMNESS, FIRST, INOPERATIVE, DEFEND.

(b) DESTRUCTION is to RUIN as INSTRUCTOR is to:

TEACHER, TUTOR, TRAINER, COACH, EDUCATOR.

(c) Consider the following list of words:

RACK, ON, GAIN, RAGE, ROW.

Now choose one of the following words to add to the list:

HEDGE, WOOD, STORM, TRACK, MAID, WATER, MILK.

(d) Fill in the missing letters and read clockwise to find the eight-letter words:

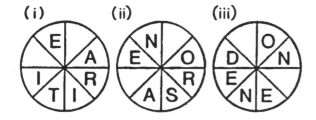

4 TEASERS

(a) A wheel is spun containing 10 red and 10 yellow equal segments. Above the wheel is an arrow. What are the chances that in any 10 consecutive spins the same color will appear against the arrow?

(b) Eight bingo balls numbered from 1 to 8 are placed into a bag then drawn out at random, one by one, and the numbers written down to form an eight-figure number. What are the odds that the eight-figure number will divide by 9 exactly?

(c) If the man who always transgressed against divine or moral law was named Dennis, the girl who always felt unwell was named Delia, and the lady who had a thing of value was named Tessa, what was the name of the man who carried a bag of letters?

(d) Jim, Alf, and Sid each win on the horses for three days running. The following are the nine amounts which the bookie paid out (starting with the largest amount to the smallest amount):

$65 $52 $47 $39 $26 $23 $21 $15 $12.

Jim won twice as much as Sid. What was the total winning amount for each man over the three days?

5 CONDITIONS

A condition is a test where you are shown one box and then asked to choose, from a list of options, which one other box meets the same conditions, e.g., which of the five boxes on the right meets the same conditions as the box on the left.

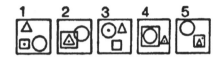

The answer is 3 because it is the only one where the dot is inside the circle. Now try the following (to increase the difficulty in A, B, and E, the dots are shown only in the left-hand box).

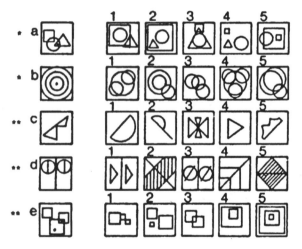

6 FAMOUS NAMES

(a) Name these all-American presidents:

(i) OH! GOING? GREAT NEWS

(ii) RAM BALL ON CHAIN

(iii) BOTH HERE ROVER

(iv) WIND OR OWLS WOO

(v) LODGE CIVIC LOAN

(vi) O DO REVERSE THE TOOL

(vii) A FOOLER SENT LINK OVERLAND

(b) Name these well-known writers:

(i) KEN SCARES CHILD

(ii) REASON ANN IT'S HARD CHINS

(iii) LOB NET OR CHATTER

(iv) NEW SMILE ESSENTIAL

(v) A BELL CHARMS

(vi) TO STEER NOON SILVER BUS

(vii) SHAME MARE MUST GO

7 NO NEIGHBORS

In each of the following, unscramble the letters to find a word. There are no two adjoining letters in the same shape.

(a) 11-letter word.

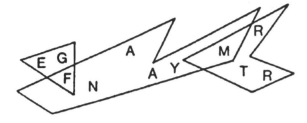

(b) 12-letter word.

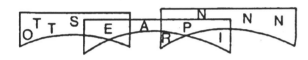

(c) 14-letter word.

8 SQUARE WORDS

Spiral clockwise around the perimeter, adding letters in the empty boxes, and finish at the center square to spell out the nine-letter words. Each word begins at one of the four corner squares.

(a)*

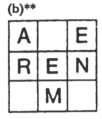

(b)**

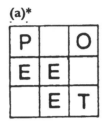

(c)*

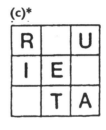

(d)***

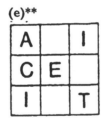

(e)**

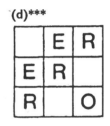

9 MATCHSTICKS

Fifty-seven matchsticks are laid out to form the sum below, which is obviously incorrect:

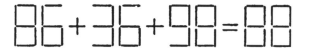

But, by removing *two* matchsticks, it is possible to make the sum correct:

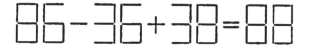

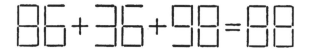

(a)** Now the same sum is laid out again, but this time remove *eight* matchsticks to make the sum correct. (Do not disturb the matchsticks already laid out, apart from the eight to be removed).

(b)* Now, for an incomplete sum. This time *add* 18 matchsticks to make the sum correct. (Do not disturb the matchsticks already laid out).

10 TWO IN ONE

In each of the following, two quotations are squashed together. All the letters are in the correct order. Find the two quotations. To assist, the authors' names follow the quotations, but have been squashed together in the same way.

(a)*

AALLLKLLENOARNWINLEDGGIESBIUST-
BRUETCREOMELMLBECRATNICOEN.

SPOCLRAATETOS

(b)** TOYOEUHARVETRWOEAISRSHE-
HARBUOTHMSIDANTESOFOFTORHE-
GIVQU EESDTIVIOINNE.

SPPOURGPEEON

11 FIND THE QUOTATIONS

In each of the following, find the starting point, fill in the missing letters, and a quotation will appear. Then rearrange the missing letters to find the author/originator of the quotation.

*(a) Author (5 letters)   *(b) Author (6 letters)

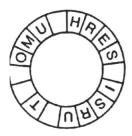   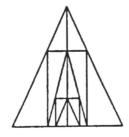

*(c) Originator (6 and 6)

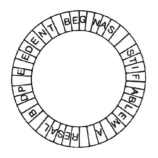

12 COUNTING TRIANGLES

How many triangles are there in each of the following figures? The number of triangles increases in each figure. The first figure is a warm-up.

(a)*   (b)***

   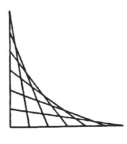

(c)***   (d)***

NOW CHECK YOUR ANSWERS AND RECORD YOUR SCORE.

I Spad. The remainder are the first three letters of a country followed by the first letter of its capital. Chile-Santiago, Denmark-Copenhagen, France-Paris, Peru-Lima, Portugal-Lisbon.

2 To fall and not touch a line, the card must fall so that the center of the card falls within the shaded area.

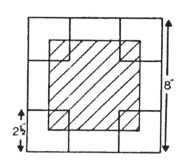 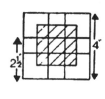

For	Against		For	Against
$30\frac{1}{4}$in.^{2}	$33\frac{3}{4}$in.^{2}		$21\frac{1}{4}$in.^{2}	$13\frac{3}{4}$in.^{2}

In the proportion I to 4

	For	Against
Therefore	$30\frac{1}{4}$	$33\frac{3}{4}$
	$2\frac{1}{4}$	$13\frac{3}{4}$
	$2\frac{1}{4}$	$13\frac{3}{4}$
	$2\frac{1}{4}$	$13\frac{3}{4}$
	$2\frac{1}{4}$	$13\frac{3}{4}$
	$39\frac{1}{4}$	$88\frac{3}{4}$

x 4 to remove fractions

	157	to	355
	For		Against

3 220 and 284; i.e., 220 + 110 + 55 + 44 + 22 + 20 + 11 + 10 + 5 + 4 + 2 +1 = 504

284 + 142 + 71 + 4 +2 + 1 = 504

1 (a) (i) P. The initial of the planets in order from the sun. Mercury, Venus, Earth, Mars, Jupiter, Saturn, Uranus, Neptune, Pluto.

(ii) X. A list of letters in the alphabet which are also Roman numerals.

(iii) S. The initials of the seven deadly sins: Pride, Wrath, Envy, Lust, Gluttony, Avarice, Sloth.

(b) T. They are initials of odd numbers: one, three, five, etc.

(c) (i) IOE. They are the vowels extracted from the colors of the rainbow: red, orange, yellow, green, blue, indigo, violet.

(ii) AUA. They are the vowels extracted from the days of the week: Sunday, Monday, Tuesday, Wednesday, Thursday, Friday, Saturday.

(d) Above the line. Straight letters go above; curved letters below.

(e) F.A.A.N. They are the initials of the months of the year.

2 (a) (i) 529, 841. They are the squares of progressive prime numbers.
(ii) 10. i.e. $9 \times 7 \times 3 \times 7 \times 6 = 7938$. $7 \times 9 \times 3 \times 8 = 1512$. $1 \times 5 \times 1 \times 2 = 10$.
(iii) 3125. i.e. 5^5. The sequence is $1^1, 2^2, 3^3, 4^4, 5^5$.
(iv) 2574. It is the odd numbers from the previous number multiplied by the even numbers, i.e., 99×26.
(v) 792. It is the square numbers from the previous number multiplied by the remaining numbers, i.e. 9×88.

(b) 857, 859. Rearrange the digits of 7731 in every possible way and then divide the resultant number by 9.

(c) $428 + 533 = 961$, $566 + 127 = 693$, $361 + 414 = 775$, $565 + 196 = 761$.

(d) 72. The number at top is one quarter of the sum of the two numbers below.

3 (a) They each contain three adjacent consecutive letters of the alphabet, e.g. *stu*dio.

(b) Tutor: its letters are contained in instructor in the correct order as with destruction/ruin.

(c) Maid. All words can be prefixed with BAR to form another word.

(d) (i) Maritime **(ii)** Forsaken **(iii)** Convened.

4 (a) One in 1024. Each spin is an even chance, i.e., 1 in 2. To repeat 10 times is 1 in 2^{10}

(b) Certainty. The sum of the digits 1-8 is 36. Any number divides by 9 exactly when the sum of its digits also divides by 9 exactly. It does not matter in which order the balls are drawn out as the sum will always be 36.

(c) Liam (i.e. Mail reversed). Dennis Sinned, Delia Ailed and Tessa has an asset.

(d) Jim wins $26 + $39 + $47 = $112; Sid wins $12 + $23 = $21 = $56; Alf wins $15 + $52 + $65 = $132.

5 (a) 3. The only one in which the dot could go in both circle and triangle.

(b) 5. The only one in which dot could go in all three circles.

(c) 2. The only one that is an asummetrical figure.

(d) 4. The only one in which the two halves of the square are a mirror image, assuming the dividing line is a mirror.

(e) 5. The only one in which one dot could go in one square only and one dot in two square only.

6 (a) (i) George Washington, **(ii)** Abraham Lincoln, **(iii)** Herbert Hoover, **(iv)** Woodrow Wilson, **(v)** Calvin Coolidge, **(vi)** Theodore Roosevelt, **(vii)** Franklin Delano Roosevelt.

(b) (i) Charles Dickens, **(ii)** Hans Christian Anderson, **(iii)** Charlotte Bronte, **(iv)** Tennessee Williams, **(v)** Charles Lamb, **(vi)** Robert Louis Stevenson, **(vii)** Somerset Maugham.

7 (a) Fragmentary, **(b)** Transpontine, **(c)** Tergiversation.

8 (a) Telephone, **(b)** Enumerate, **(c)** Circulate, **(d)** Reservoir, **(e)** Intricate.

9 (a)

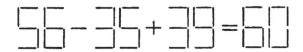

(b)

10 (a) All knowledge is but remembrance. —Plato

All learning is but recollection. —Socrates

(b) To err is human, to forgive, divine. —Pope

You have two ears; hear both sides of the question. —Spurgeon

11 (a) Too much rest is rust. —Walter Scott

(b) Old friends are best. —John Selden

(c) All bad precedents began as justifiable measures. —Julius Caesar

12 (a) 23, **(b)** 59, **(c)** 105, **(d)** 111.

SCORING

THE PUBLISHER'S SCORING INSTRUCTIONS

Count up the number of correct answers you received in the tests in each of the Elementary, Challenging and/or Masterful test levels. Find your approximate IQ score in the extreme right hand column. You may measure your IQ after one category of tests, or look to the sum of your scores for each of the test levels for your composite score after you have completed all three test levels.

NOTE: This chart is based on test-takers who are 16 years or older. If you are younger than 16, add 10 points to your score for every year your age falls below 16.

ELEMENTARY	CHALLENGING	MASTERFUL	COMPOSITE	YOUR IQ
147	159	62	368	170
144	156	61	361	168
141	153	60	354	166
138	150	58.5	346.5	164
135	147	58	340	162
132	144	57	333	160
129	141	56.5	326.5	158
126	138	55	319	156
123	135	54.5	312.5	154
120	132	53	305	152
117	129	52	298	150
114	126	50	290	148
111	123	48	282	146
108	120	46	274	144
105	117	44	266	142
102	114	42	258	140
99	111	40	250	138
96	108	38	242	136
93	105	36	234	134
90	102	34	226	132
87	99	32	218	130
84	96	30	210	128
81	93	28	202	126
78	90	26	194	124
75	87	24	186	122
72	84	22	178	120
69	81	20	170	118
66	78	18	162	116
63	75	16	154	114
60	72	14	146	112
57	69	12	138	110
54	66	10	130	108
51	63	8	122	106
48	60	6	114	104
45	57	4	106	102
42	54	2	98	100

THE PUBLISHER'S SCORING INSTRUCTIONS

Count up the number of correct answers you received in the tests in each of the Comprehensive Supertests. Find your approximate IQ score in the extreme right hand column. You may measure your IQ after one test, or look to the sum of your scores for each of the tests for your composite score after you have completed all three test levels.

NOTE: This chart is based on test-takers who are 16 years or older. If you are younger than 16, add 10 points to your score for every year your age falls below 16.

SUPERTEST I	SUPERTEST II	COMPOSITE	YOUR IQ
30	42	72	185
29	41	70	184
28	40	68	183
27	39	66	182
26	38	64	181
25	37	62	180
24	36	60	179
23	35	58	178
22	34	56	177
21	33	54	176
20	32	52	175
19	31	50	174
18	30	48	173
17	29	46	172
16	28	44	171
15	27	42	170
14	26	40	169
13	25	38	168
12	24	36	167
11	23	34	166
10	22	32	165
9	21	30	164
8	20	28	163
7	19	26	162
6	18	24	161
5	17	22	160
4	16	20	159
3	15	18	158
2	14	16	157
1	13	14	156